BEFORE YOUR JOURNEY

A PREMARITAL STUDY GUIDE

DR. MAX W. REAMS

COMPANION BOOK:

ON THE JOURNEY
A MARRIED COUPLE'S
STUDY GUIDE

Good marriages do not just happen. They must be nurtured and carefully maintained. Two key elements needed to develop and sustain a good marriage are communication and a shared spiritual life. With that in mind, Dr. Max Reams provides a rich set of devotionals that will help couples enrich their marriage relationship. These 60 daily devotionals are designed to assist couples as they cultivate the habit of sharing a daily devotional time. Dr. Reams' words are practical, biblical, and time-tested in his own marriage and in countless counseling sessions with young couples. These devotionals have wide appeal. I highly recommend *Before Your Journey*.

Dr. John C. Bowling, President, Olivet Nazarene University

We don't know of a professor who has had more impact over more years at Olivet than Dr. Max Reams. His five decades of teaching have not been limited to his classroom, however. All of us who are fortunate enough to know Max have benefited from the passion he and Carol share for ministering to couples on our campus and beyond. That's why this resource is so eagerly anticipated. Consider it your roadmap for an incredible journey of walking together with God. Packed with inspiration and biblical wisdom, this resource will help the two of you join your spirits like never before.

Drs. Les & Leslie Parrott, #1 New York Times bestselling authors of *Saving Your Marriage Before It Starts*

Each of the 60-day readings in *Before Your Journey* is brimming with relational wisdom and scriptural truth balanced with contemporary research and resources. The result will jumpstart your marital journey toward a healthy and joyous path. Here is a book you will treasure!

David J. Wine, Discipleship Pastor, GatheringPoint Church of the Nazarene and Associate Professor of Christian Ministry, Olivet Nazarene University

BACKGROUND

These devotionals are modified from thoughts shared in classes when I taught at Olivet Nazarene University. This book is a response to student requests that the thoughts become available in print. Additional material is drawn from retreats for married couples, led by my wife, Carol Reams, and me. This collection is not intended in any way to replace premarital counseling or therapy. Nor are all topics related to premarriage or marriage discussed. My hope is that this material may assist couples' devotional time and discussions and also encourage them to seek premarital counseling with a trained counselor or pastor.

Copyright © 2019 by Max W. Reams

All rights reserved.

ISBN: 9781080211807

Independently Published.

Scripture quotations from the New International Version Bible (NIV)

Cover Photo: Courtesy of Joe Mantarian

Cover Design: Randall Rupert

DISCLAIMER

The information provided in this book is for inspirational purposes only; it is not intended nor implied to be a substitute for professional premarital or marital advice, counseling, diagnosis, or treatment. Always consult a premarital or marital professional with any questions you may have prior to making a decision regarding the information based on what you have read in this book. Never disregard professional advice, or delay in seeking it, because of something you have read in this book or in the content of the links or references in the content resources. The author does not endorse nor necessarily agree with information in the linked resources or references.

ACKNOWLEDGMENTS

I am thankful to the staff of Olivet Nazarene University's Office of Institutional Advancement for their heartfelt support to help make this book possible. I am grateful to my editor, Laura Warfel, and to my thoughtful and insightful volunteer readers. Barbara Axmark provided insight regarding formatting. Randall Rupert gave important assistance with layout and other details. I appreciate everyone for their excellent suggestions and careful work. Their contributions have greatly improved the text. All errors are mine.

DEDICATION

This book is dedicated to Carol, my wife and chief encourager, without whom this book would never have seen the light of day, and to our children, grandchildren, and great-grandchildren.

HOW TO USE THIS BOOK

These 60 devotionals are designed to be read by couples after referring to the scripture references cited. Questions are provided to assist in discussion. Prayer points and take-aways are for further thought. The devotionals are arranged in a degree of order, but most can be read as stand-alone entities. Space is provided for notes and responses.

TABLE OF CONTENTS

-1-

WHAT ATTRACTS ONE PERSON TO ANOTHER?

Read: Song of Songs 1:15 and 1:16a

Focus: "How beautiful you are, my darling! Oh, how beautiful! Your eyes are doves." . . . "How handsome you are, my lover! Oh, how charming!"

Studies dealing with what initially attracts one person to another usually list physical attraction as one of the beginning factors. There is no universal understanding of what is physically attracting for couples, since superficial appearance is only one possibility. Physical appearance often is just a prelude to discover what the person is like in other ways. Sometimes the attraction has little to do with perceived beauty or handsomeness.

As an outsider looking on, you may have wondered what attracted some couples you have known. Perhaps the attraction had little to do with what our culture defines as visual attractiveness. The magnet may have been aesthetic, such as between two people who share a common love for music or art. Others are attracted because they share a common goal, purpose, interest, or religious perspective. The possibilities are endless!

Attraction can occur between people who come from similar backgrounds. This explains why individuals who live near each other are often attracted together. Similar family patterns and expectations can also draw one person to another. It is no surprise

1

that many individuals find themselves attracted to their fellow classmates in high school or college. Others meet in work settings that arise from common career pursuits. Those of similar cultural backgrounds, whether regional or local, may find comfortable connections. Shared religious experiences can be attractive, especially for committed believers.

Personality similarities or differences also play a role in some attractions. Feeling relaxed in the presence of another may be attractive, whether due to commonalities or unlike characteristics. Opposites often attract, but so do nearly identical personalities.

Once there is an initial attraction, that may be all there is! In order for a couple to take their relationship seriously and allow it to grow, they have a lot of work to do. Otherwise, the beginning connection may fizzle and they separate. Other characteristics may be discovered that nix a meaningful and happy long-term relationship. For many, that would be a good thing! From the beginning of your relationship, learn all you can about what makes a meaningful relationship.*

Resource:
The DNA of Relationships, Gary Smalley, Tyndale House Publishers.

Discussion Questions:
1. Describe the attractions each of you felt for the other when you first met.

2. Describe the current attractions you feel for each other. Be specific.

3. Describe how these attractions have the potential to make your relationship grow.

Prayer Point/Take Away for Today:
Think about the most important personality characteristic(s)
he/she possesses.

Notes/Responses/Action:

-2-

DATING: WHY BOTHER?

There are no biblical scriptures directly related to dating, since dating is a modern Western cultural arrangement.

Read: Genesis 24:57–67

Focus: Note the progression of an arranged marriage. Deeply devoted love occurred *after* marriage!

What is the purpose of dating? For a couple who are initially attracted, dating allows them to discover what relating with the opposite gender is like. This can be huge for both women and men. Regardless of one's family background and non-romantic male-female connections, dating provides an opportunity to deal with a unique difference of the sexes: communication. Women and men generally communicate in rather different ways.* More about that later.

Dating is not a trial engagement, nor is it a trial marriage! Dating should be considered as a way of learning to communicate with someone of the opposite gender. Talking should dominate the dating scene.

Premarital sex short-circuits the process of discovery of each other's uniquenesses. The media have ruined a perfectly wonderful method of coming to better understand opposite genders by presuming that having sex should be part of dating. This is based on a hedonistic approach to life, where physical individualistic pleasure is all-important. God's plan from the

4

beginning put sexual intimacy within marriage. There is so much more to this plan than quick connection, temporary stimulus, and sexual gratification.

Communication should be the focus of dating, since this is the most critical piece of any relationship. If groping and sexual acts enter the dating phase of a relationship, then a couple faces the likelihood of inadequate preparation for a future long-term connection. The one night stand becomes just that, with little hope of any mature development and understanding of each other. A successful marital relationship must be grounded in effective communication.

There is a second value of dating: to have fun with someone who is unlike you in many ways. Guys have fun doing whatever guys like to do, and gals likewise enjoy the company of other women. Dating is unlike those relationships. Dating forces gender differences into the open to help discover fun that both can enjoy. Couples can learn how to participate in shared experiences that neither might have considered before.

Basically, dating should be a learning and enjoyable time. But here is the warning: don't become serious too soon! Yes, dating can be a prelude to more serious things, such as finding a soulmate, but let that play out in the background. Don't force the relationship. Let things develop naturally and (usually) slowly! Dating is not engagement and should involve no long-term commitment. Take your time.

Some people date only the person they eventually marry, but this is unusual and not the norm. Dating more than one person allows you to eventually become serious about one person from a base of understanding.

You should not be forced into a relationship guided by the expectations of peers or relatives who have your life planned out for you. Just because you have had one or two dates with someone does not mean that you are as serious as your friends suppose!

Enjoy dating. Hopefully this experience will help you avoid the pain of a rapid engagement and too-quick marriage, followed by discouragement and a tragic divorce. Dating should set the stage for eventually finding your real soulmate.

Carefully consider your approach to dating. Be certain to carry your Christian faith with you.**

Resources:
You Just Don't Understand, Deborah Tannen, Ballantine Books.
**https://www.biblestudytools.com/blogs/stephen-altrogge/4-rules-to-simplify-christian-dating.html

Discussion Questions:

1. Describe how each of you defines fun.

2. Make a list of fun things you can do together. Be creative!

3. Choose something this week that would be fun for both of you and do it.

Prayer Point/Take Away for Today:
Consider doing something that she/he thinks is fun but maybe I don't.

Notes/Responses/Action:

(Continued)

Notes/Responses/Action:

-3-

SHOULD YOU MARRY?

Read: Genesis 2:24; 1 Corinthians 7; 1 Timothy 5;
Matthew 19:4–6

Focus: God clearly indicates the normal pattern for most of us is
to marry. Critiquing easy divorce in the Jewish population, Jesus
referred this loose approach to marriage back to Genesis 2:24 as
an antidote. St. Paul lived in a pagan society where all sorts of
sexual behavior threatened to influence New Testament Christian
behavior. He wrestled with how these early Christians could best
deal with marriage, divorce, and singularity in 1 Corinthians,
chapter 7, and 1 Timothy, chapter 5. If modern studies of the
value of marriage mean anything, they reinforce Genesis 2:24 as
the standard for healthy marital relationships.

Not everyone should marry. Why? There are many reasons
for remaining single. Some areas of service, both secular and
religious, may best be done by singles. The lifestyle of singles
may permit activities and time to do what marrieds cannot do as
effectively.

Unfortunately, too often our churches and society in
general relegate the single life to the back burner of existence.
Governments provide benefits to married individuals that singles
don't receive. Churches too frequently give preference to married
persons within their systems. Jesus (Matthew 19:4–6) and St. Paul
certainly did not approve of this relegation of unmarried persons

to second-class status. The celibate life should not be penalized but treated with respect.

The Bible indicates that most Christians will marry and will serve both God and society as a result. Your choice of a marriage partner should be in the light of scripture. Christians should marry each other, or they face the pain of spiritual incompatibility. It is always fair to ask yourself if the person you are considering for marriage is a believer. Shared religious beliefs and experience is very important, but don't assume that a faith connection is the only key to a happy marital relationship.

Discussion Questions:
1. Are there ways you have felt isolated as a single? If so, how have you dealt with this?

2. Describe how you connect with singles and marrieds on a social level.

3. What are things you, as a couple, can do to explore your religious connection?

Prayer Point/Take Away for Today:
Evaluate my spiritual connections and responsibilities.

Notes/Responses/Action:

(Continued)

Notes/Responses/Action:

IS GOD INVOLVED IN YOUR SELECTION OF A MARRIAGE PARTNER?

Read: Genesis 24:1–67

Focus: This is one of the most interesting love stories in the Old Testament. It involves an amazing account of how God directed Abraham's servant to discover Rebekah and bring her to marry Isaac.

If you decide to marry, will God direct you to just the right person? There are few teachings in the Bible about specifically whom you should marry. The lineage leading to Jesus from Abraham and King David had to be preserved, so those marriages were recorded by Matthew and Luke. Jewish people have traditionally held to the Old Testament standard where God told the Israelites not to marry Gentiles living in the Promised Land. Why? Because this would draw people away from their faith. New Testament Christians were also taught to marry fellow believers. To those already married to non-believers, St. Paul generally discouraged divorce since the Christian's faithfulness might result in conversion of their spouse.

Of the more than 3.5 billion individuals on Earth of your opposite gender, how do you find *the one*? Or is there just one?

A friend of mine was walking down the sidewalk with another friend. He glanced across to the opposite side of the street and said, of a young lady whom he had never seen before, "I'm going to marry her." And he did! That is unusual, to say the least.

What if you are walking along and you happen to turn your head so you miss *the one*? Are you doomed to never find just who God has prepared and chosen for you? (This is said "tongue in cheek," of course!) We know that we serve a God of the second chance, and the third chance, and so forth. But how do you recognize one of the *chances?*

Perhaps these are all the wrong questions! The New Testament is much less about choosing a mate and much more about fulfilling the will of God. The emphasis of New Testament scripture is on pursuing a life reflecting the image of Jesus. Our decisions should align with this goal. Choosing a marriage partner fits well into this pursuit. If you and your significant other assist each other in working toward that goal, then it is possible that you might be soulmates!

So, perhaps your job is to find your soulmate! Now all you have to know is how to do that!

Discussion Questions:
1. How have you sensed God leading you in a phase of your life?

2. What does it mean to you to become more like Jesus?

3. How important is decision-making in your life? In what ways?

Prayer Point/Take Away for Today:
Pray together for guidance about our decision to date and possibly to marry.

Warning: Avoid over-spiritualizing your relationship. Don't assume the role of God!

Notes/Responses/Action:

-5-

WHAT IS A SOULMATE?

Read: Ephesians 5:31–33

Focus: These verses are the crowning summary of how a married couple is to relate to each other. And they probably include the best definition of soulmates found in the Bible.

If Christian soulmates are people who assist each other in fulfilling the will of God in their lives, then finding such a person should be an exciting adventure! What does your soulmate look like? Sorry, it's unlikely you will magically find her/his photo on your digital device.

If you are serious about locating such a person, you might go through **five stages of dating** (assuming you follow a Western culture style of dating) and eventually learn to fulfill **five basic needs** in each other's lives.

What are the **five stages of dating?***

Stage 1: Attraction. In dating, this is the getting-to-know-you step. There should be lots of talking and listening and very preliminary evaluating involved. Start out casually, without serious intent. If a closeness starts to develop and you sense an in-tune relationship beginning, cautiously begin to evaluate how you relate to this person. Ask questions. Do you communicate reasonably well together? Do you find yourself thinking how it would be to share life together (**Warning:** Don't push this to the front too soon.)? How can you assist this person in her/his life in

14

Christ? We will explore lots of other questions in future devotionals.

Stage 2: Uncertainty. This is a questioning phase that centers heavily on the rightness you and she/he are seeking in each other. Don't rush past this period of questioning. Evaluate your thoughts and emotions. It is easy to dash ahead, but take time to linger in this in-between domain. You may need to clear your head and remove the rose-colored glasses long enough to think clearly. I've known individuals who jumped this phase and went straight to marriage. That is often a serious mistake, and pain may lie ahead. By clearly evaluating the relationship now, you could walk away and avoid a disastrous divorce later.

Stage 3: Exclusivity. This can be defined in many ways. The term(s) used vary with age and society's expectations. Basically, exclusivity means that a couple can relax and share without competition. This does not suggest that you do things only as a couple. Group activities are part of the entire dating process and stages. An added advantage of spending time with other couples and single friends is the opportunity they have of observing and evaluating the suitability of your special person and you. It may seem odd, but ask them how they see the two of you together. Don't be upset if you get a negative response. They may see what you cannot. Not that you let others decide whom you should love, but at least hear the input others have for you.

Exclusivity is not a guarantee that you will avoid breaking up and going your separate ways! It just assures that you have both agreed not to date others while you are together. Why be exclusive? The purpose is to remove the competition, at least on a temporary basis. You need to focus on learning more about each other. This is very much a time to evaluate who you are as a couple and think about future possibilities.

Stage 4: Intimacy. This is a time to let down your guard and explore who you really are. Don't confuse this stage with the media's use of the word *intimacy*, which too often refers to having sex. At this stage, sex can definitely get in the way of your finding out more about each other as you unmask your inner selves. Becoming more transparent is key in this phase. Some of the skeletons in your closets may need to be delicately discussed. This is **not** a therapy situation; that is reserved for professionals. Revealing issues that might get in the way of building your relationship is important. Be aware that intimacy may bring out information that might prevent your moving on to the next stage. You can still break up here. That might be the best thing to happen. This is not necessarily a warm, fuzzy phase. Both of you will likely discover that each has feet of clay, that is, that you are human and imperfect.

Stage 5: Engagement. This phase involves sharing future plans and resolving disagreements and disappointments, even if an engagement ring is not involved. Think beyond the giddy picture of the spectacular party congratulating you as the newly engaged couple. Engagement needs to be a serious time for couples as they wrestle with what they are discovering about each other. There ought to be some important discussions about finances, careers, family commitments, and irritating character imperfections that each of you has. The rose-colored glasses should begin to clear up as you see each other with sharpened clarity, warts and all!

By all means, the engagement stage is the time to see a pastor or counselor for premarital counseling, if you haven't already. The hours and whatever costs may be involved are well worth it to experience in-depth interaction under the guidance of a third party. A premarital assessment tool should be part of this process.

Regardless of how deeply you go into the engagement stage, there is still time to bail out. Yes, there might be embarrassment involved and a ring returned, but better that than a messy divorce later. This phase is not meant to be brutal or discouraging, but it is a time to really see each other as the couple you might become in the future. It can be very exciting and beneficial. Couples who take engagement seriously have a much higher success rate of having a happy marriage that lasts. Move through all of the stages. Skipping a stage can sow the seeds for later disaster. What is the hurry? Take your time. Sex? Wait. It will be worth it on your wedding night!

Resource:
*www.ehcounseling.com/materials/relationship_5_stage.pdf

Discussion Questions:
1. Which stage do each of you see yourselves in right now? How do you know?

2. What is most important to think about in the stage where you are right now? Why?

3. What do you need to do to move on to the next stage, if that is your goal? Are there red flags that you need to heed before continuing your present relationship?

Prayer Point/Take Away for Today:
What is my responsibility in working through the dating stage we are in right now?

Notes/Responses/Action:

(Continued)

Notes/Responses/Action:

-6-

HOW NOT TO DISCOVER A SOULMATE

Reread: Ephesians 5:31–33

Focus: Soulmates are essential in marriage.

The person you marry is one of life's most important decisions, probably second only to your decision to accept Christ as Savior. Some people become desperate to find that ideal soulmate and end up making serious mistakes.

Here are a few ways **not** to find a soulmate:*

1. Look in the wrong places. It might be possible to find that special person anywhere. I have heard of some bizarre locations! Consider the type of person you are interested in. Would you likely find her/him in a singles bar or in a church? Online or through a friend? In some places, you are more likely to strike gold while in others you may find only fool's gold.

2. Date someone until you or they are resentful. Some relationships are just not meant to be. If one member of the couple picks up on this and the other does not, resentments can make things unpleasant. Better to break it off kindly than to make both of you miserable.

3. Manipulate someone. There is a false premise, too often held, that we can change someone to become like the image we wish them to be. This never works. The only person we can change is ourselves.

4. Break up in anger. Sometimes emotions can get carried too far. Do your best to catch things before tempers flare to the boiling point. Either call a temporary pause in the relationship or agree to end amicably. It is possible to retain some degree of friendship, even after a breakup. Good endings can pave the way for a better beginning with another person. You may have already learned through a breakup who is not your soulmate.

5. Repeat the above mistakes and hope that the result will be different. This myth needs to be replaced with a new reality. Perhaps your approach or attitude should change.

Resource:
*http://booksums.blogspot.com/2008/04/mars-and-venus-on-date-john-gray.html

Discussion Questions:
1. Describe the first time you met. Be detailed.

2. Consider sharing negative dating experiences you might have had or ones your friends have experienced. What can you learn from these?

3. If you think you might be soulmates, what suggests this is so? Or what suggests you might question that you are soulmates?

Prayer Point/Take Away for Today:
If I am to be somebody's soulmate, what are my responsibilities?

Notes/Responses/Action:

(Continued)

Notes/Responses/Action:

-7-

BASIC NEEDS

Read: James 2:18, 3:13

Focus: Our actions need to match what we say. How we relate to each other is key to building a solid relationship.

Those who study human behavior often note the basic relational needs we all possess.* As a premarried couple, you cannot provide for all the needs of your significant other at this stage in your relationship. Following are areas of need that could eventually develop, especially after marriage.

Physical needs: Beyond our needs for water, food, shelter, etc., the physical presence of others is essential in our lives. As previously mentioned, we are often attracted by the appearance of someone. But be aware: our physical appearance changes. Wrinkles appear! Gravity works on our bodies, and various features so attractive in our 20s give way to sagging. Change will happen, but the amazing thing is this: physical attraction can last a lifetime if emotional, mental, social, and spiritual needs are also met. That is why it is important to look beyond body shape and outward beauty.

In a marital relationship, there are many physical needs that spouses must satisfy for the other person. Sexual intimacy is designed to help bond a couple together. Equally important are acts of service to each other. This spans a wide spectrum and includes meal preparation, laundry, home and vehicle maintenance, child care, household cleaning, and a host of other needs a couple must deal with on a daily basis.

Life can settle into a routine, and it is all too common that couples begin to take each other's physical needs for granted. Meeting each other's needs as time passes is very important. Honest discussion about expectations and personal concerns can go a long way toward helping each other meet the demands of life. More about this in later devotionals.

Emotional needs: Each person needs to feel loved, and your significant other is the most important person with this need. Love is locally defined, that is, everyone recognizes love in their own way. Later, we will discuss these love needs in more detail. To meet your partner's emotional needs in a relationship requires that you maintain focus and be sensitive to what he/she is all about. Love is not satisfied once a week or only on Valentine's Day. We are all needy people, and to meet the love needs of each other is one of our most important relational concerns. Ask questions often. Never accept "fine" or "okay" as a response to a question.

Mental or brain needs: Everyone needs mental stimulation in some form. Discover what stimulates the brain of your significant other and feed that domain. The range of mental interests is wide: reading, finances, sports, academic, building, art, music, crafts, hobbies, repairs, or whatever. Encourage each other to develop brain activities. If you have something in common here, emphasize that to build a relational connection. Take a class together. Build something together. The more you can connect mentally, the stronger will be your bond.

Social needs: No one is an island, and the same is true for a couple. Make connections with other couples. Develop group connections. Become part of a couples' small group at a church. In addition, encourage each other to connect individually with others of your gender, a political organization, a service club, or some group that interests you. This helps prevent a couple from becoming too dependent on each other.

Spiritual needs: Develop your spiritual lives by sharing devotional and prayer times together. Encourage individual spiritual development. Attend and become involved in church and other organizations with a spiritual emphasis. Spiritual bonding can be a powerful glue to hold your relationship together, especially during difficult times. **Warning:** Sharing intimate spiritual experiences can lead to intimate sexual experiences. Be cautious in this area.

Resource:
*http://booksums.blogspot.com/2008/04/mars-and-venus-on-date-john-gray.html

Discussion Questions:
1. How would you describe some of your physical, emotional, mental, social, or spiritual needs?

2. What do you consider your most significant need? Why?

3. How could you begin to meet one of his/her needs?

Prayer Point/Take Away for Today:
What is a need I can focus on meeting for her/him?

Notes/Responses/Action:

(Continued)

Notes/Responses/Action:

-8-

WHAT ARE YOUR CRITERIA FOR A LIFE PARTNER?

Read: Galatians 5:22–26

Focus: Seek high virtues in a marriage partner.

It is impossible to list all the characteristics or concerns that one might consider important when seeking a marriage partner, but here are a few to consider.

1. Spiritual compatibility
2. Personality
3. Social-cultural backgrounds
4. Economic status
5. Financial savvy
6. Interests
7. Goals
8. Habits
9. Education
10. Interpersonal skills: conflict resolution
11. Interpersonal issues: anger, jealousy
12. Myths: romanticisms
13. Myths: roles
14. Gender bias and attitudes
15. Food skills and preferences
16. (Add your own ideas!)

This list should make it obvious that there is a lot to talk about when you're dating, as opposed to spending all your time in physical contact.

Watch out for love at first sight as a sole criterion for developing a relationship. Mark Ballenger* observes that this turned out well with Rebekah and Isaac (Genesis 24:62–67) and with Rachel and Jacob (Genesis 29:1–12), but it failed miserably for David and Bathsheba (2 Samuel 11 and 12) and Amnon and Tamar (2 Samuel 13). Initial attraction is just that: initial.

Resource:
*http://applygodsword.com/what-does-the-bible-say-about-love-at-first-sight/

Discussion Questions:
1. Choose one of the characteristics above and describe yourself in those terms.

2. Are there changes you would like to make in this characteristic?

3. Choose another of these personal characteristics and describe yourself in those terms.

4. Are there changes you would like to make in this characteristic?

Prayer Point/Take Away for Today:
How do I see myself as a person with desirable characteristics? How can God help me here?

Notes/Responses/Action:

(Continued)

Notes/Responses/Action:

-9-

FAITH FACTORS

Read: Matthew 22:37–39

Focus: The challenge of life and your relationship is to live out these amazing commandments.

How important is faith in a couple's relationship? According to St. Paul and the Bible in general: choosing a life partner who is a believer is very important. If your personal faith is a significant part of your life, then being able to share your spiritual life with your spouse is integral to a happy relationship.

Why is this spiritual connection important? For Christians, the spiritual life is more than an add-on to life as a whole. Faith is the foundation on which all of life is based. Christians view our earthly lives as a place to show love to others and emulate the life of Jesus.

But what is involved in the spiritual life? As a person who has personally accepted Jesus Christ as your personal Savior, the new life God gives you is one that involves faith with the Holy Spirit as your guide. Common features of a Christian believer's life include: reading the Bible; praying; and interacting with other believers, often through a church setting. Involvement in outreach activities may include service through church, charitable organizations, school programs, or a wide variety of groups.

How compatible should a couple be spiritually? This is an important matter for premarrieds to discuss. Some people look for

29

anyone who at least professes faith or hopefully goes to church. Certainly these are starters, but will they be enough to satisfy your need for a rich, shared spiritual experience?

Same church or denomination? There is more than the name on the church door to bring peace to a relationship.

What is your worldview? How do you spend your spare time? How alike are your lifestyles? How do you view people, especially those unlike yourself racially, politically, culturally, or economically? How do you view the importance of the scriptures, prayer, and your witness? These should be explored in premarital counseling, along with many other topics.

Don't seek a clone of yourself. That would be boring! But your faithfulness to God, concern for the world, and love of family are very important characteristics that you probably want to have in a relationship. One of the especially meaningful activities that Christian couples can experience is a shared devotional time. This often involves scripture reading and prayer. A devotional book or guide may help. In addition, Christians usually find a personal time to pray and read scripture.

As a believing couple, doing a service or ministry activity together can be a very enriching experience. This allows sharing commonly held prayer concerns and mutual support. Having a shared faith also involves financial support for faith-based organizations.

You both come from different family and personal spiritual backgrounds. Attending the same church does not guarantee spiritual oneness. Seeing the world and God from a similar point of view is the most important thing.

Talk about your faith with your significant other. Pray for each other. And take the building of your relationship seriously*.

Warning: Intense spiritual activities, such as prayer, are often so intimate that couples are drawn together sexually. You might want to hold off on the intensity level until after the marriage vows!

Resource:
Saving Your Marriage Before It Starts, Les Parrott III and Leslie Parrott, Zondervan.

Discussion Questions:
1. Describe your faith background, in detail.

2. What are some goals of your spiritual life? Be specific.

3. Describe what you look for when you meet people. Do you consider yourself biased toward other groups? If so, why?

4. What changes might take place in your spiritual lives, if you decide to marry?

Prayer Point/Take Away for Today:
Offer a prayer for her/his spiritual development.

Notes/Responses/Action:

(Continued)

Notes/Responses/Action:

-10-

FORGIVENESS

Read: Matthew 18:21–26; Ephesians 5:25–31

Focus: Jesus taught unlimited forgiveness between believers. Paul taught that sacrificial forgiveness is part of the marital bond.

No one is perfect. If each of you looks for someone who is perfect, you will both be disappointed! Better to seek to understand each other.*

How forgiving are you and your potential life partner? We are all imperfect beings and need to live with the forgiveness attitude of Jesus. In response to how many times we should forgive the same person, Jesus gave an outlandish number: 490 times! In no way did Jesus want us to count up to 490 and then stop forgiving. He was teaching the principle of forgiveness that was so missing in the culture of His day. Since God has an infinite capacity to forgive, we are to emulate God by living a life of forgiveness.

Jesus went on to say that we should love others in the way we have been loved by God and should love ourselves as well. That also translates to forgiveness for others and ourselves, too. The underlying basis for Christianity is the self-sacrifice of Jesus for us. In Jesus, God loved so much that He would do death for our forgiveness.

So, when it comes to forgiving your significant other, the standard is straightforward: Jesus' forgiveness of you. The next

33

time you have forgiven 489 times, pause and forget about counting!

Of course, Jesus did not intend for anyone to take advantage of another's forgiveness for their own benefit. When purposeful injury — whether physical, mental, emotional, or you name it — is put on another, this is wrong and requires admission and change on the part of the perpetrator. Sacrificial living goes both ways!

There is a word that comes into play here: *grace*. Philip Yancey describes God's grace this way: "Grace means that no mistake we make in life disqualifies us from God's love ... Grace is irrational, unfair, unjust, and only makes sense if I believe in another world governed by a merciful God who offers another chance."** If grace is applied between two people, think how amazing the relationship will be!

Resources:
The 7 Habits of Highly Effective People, Stephen R. Covey, A Fireside Book, Simon and Schuster (Chapter 5: Seek first to understand, then to be understood).
**Grace Notes*, Philip Yancey, Zondervan.

Discussion Questions:
1. Describe your understanding of forgiveness.

2. How have you practiced forgiveness toward each other?

3. What part might forgiveness play in a marriage?

Prayer Point/Take Away for Today:
Is there someone I need to forgive? What is the next step I need to take in that forgiveness?

Notes/Responses/Action:

-11-

ABUSE ISSUES

Read: 1 Peter 3:8–9

Focus: The Christ-like response to problems is never abusive.

We all have backgrounds that are anything but perfect. Some have seriously abusive backgrounds.*

The abuse may involve physical violence, emotional or mental abuse, sexual exploitation, and/or substance abuse (drugs, alcohol, and tobacco). Ignoring these abusive issues is unwise and can be dangerous. Abusive language and bullying are common experiences many of us have suffered in school.

To become involved in promiscuous sex is not an uncommon peer pressure in schools. Sex imposed by older relatives on children can be devastating in the memory of the exploited. Experimentation with addictive substances of all kinds can induce prolonged dependence and ruin physical, emotional, spiritual, and mental health.

If you or your significant other is plagued by any abusive issue and have not sought help, then the wisest thing to do is to find a healthcare provider, organization, support group, or counselor to assist in dealing with the issue(s). Otherwise, abusive backgrounds can color lives for years and impact future generations. Trying to go it alone is unwise; support is very important.

Resources:
*https://www.healthline.com/health/mental-health/effects-of-emotional-abuse#find-a-professional
*https://www.drugabuse.gov/publications/health-consequences-drug-misuse/mental-health-effects

Discussion Question:
1. Consider discussing abusive issues, if this seems appropriate at this time in your relationship.

Alert: If there are unresolved abusive issues, seek professional help.

Prayer Point/Take Away for Today:
Are there abuse issues I need to deal with? Has each of us moved on from those negatives in our lives, or is there still unresolved baggage?

Notes/Responses/Action:

(Continued)

Notes/Responses/Action:

-12-

VIOLENCE

Read: James 3:17–18; Proverbs 3:31; 1 Timothy 3:3

Focus: Christians avoid violence.

Violence is a topic that no one wants to think about when considering marriage. The widespread physical abuse that occurs in some relationships, however, demands that we don't ignore the problem.

Suppression of one gender for the benefit of the other has been all too common throughout human history. In most cultures, women have received the brunt of such abuse. You have probably seen this portrayed again and again in movies and television.

Violent tendencies can occur in either gender, but societal acceptance of gender dominance fosters expressions of violence by men more often than by women. Think how long it has taken in a democratic society like the United States for women to be allowed to vote and gain a variety of social, economic, and political equalities and independence.

In Western cultures, abusive violence is becoming less acceptable. This more restrictive environment may be partly responsible for violence not showing its ugly head until *after* the wedding ceremony. Potentially abusive persons may appear very nice during courtship. This may only delay violent expressions. How many have said, "If I only knew what kind of a person you were before we were married." Be alert for violent tendencies in a potential spouse. There is no magic whiffle dust that the pastor sprinkles on him or her at the marriage ceremony. You get what you get! So do your best to know what you're getting!

There is professional help for abusers, but they must be willing to accept it. Change can be slow and difficult. Look before you sign the marriage certificate! Why does anyone abuse someone so close to them? Sometimes the abuser was abused as a child or teen. This may require significant professional intervention to resolve.

For the abused person, the threat to leave the relationship often follows a tortuous path. The abuser may blame the abused for the behavior or may threaten him/her if he/she leaves. Sometimes the abuser may say the spouse can't exist without him/her. Threats may involve financial, emotional, or physical responses.

If the abused leaves, apparent penitence by the abuser may be accompanied by promises to change. But Mr./Mrs. Nice Guy may return with flowers, gifts, etc., but no fundamental change has taken place. Then the cycle may repeat itself. The threats can be real if the abused does not return. Fifty percent of the women murdered in the United States are killed by their intimate partners. Only 12 percent are murdered by strangers.*

Men kill women for a variety of reasons, but jealousy is a common one. Women tend to murder more for financial or love reasons.** Of course, women can physically abuse men. I have heard of some wicked physical abuse by women!

All this discussion may seem morbid, but abuse is far too common to ignore. Most likely, you will marry someone who is not a violent person. Before you decide to marry, be alert for any violent tendencies in him/her or in extended families.

Resources:
*www.theatlantic.com/health/archive/2017/07/homicides-women/534306/ \
**www.abc.net.au/news/2018-02-05/female-murderers-more-likely-motivated-by-love-financial-gain/9378404

Discussion Questions:
1. What are some hints that a person might be violently abusive?

2. What part might faith play in dealing with someone who is physically abusive?

Note: If there is a history of violence in your families of origin that you want to discuss, this might best be done in the presence of a counselor.

Prayer Point/Take Away for Today:
Violence will have no part in our relationships.

Notes/Responses/Action:

(Continued)

Notes/Responses/Action:

-13-

ABUSIVE WORDS

Read: Proverbs 12:16–19; Colossians 4:6; Ephesians 4:29

Focus: Use positive words, never abusive ones.

Abuse takes many forms. The more subtle abuse that is far too common involves the use of words. Words are the most efficient and clearest form of human communication. Well-chosen words can hinder or help the connection between people.

Note: The comments on gender differences are highly generalized and should not be applied to individuals.

Women have been noted to use verbal abuse very expertly on men. This can be devastating to a male partner. Verbal abuse is not the same as goofy banter that men sometimes engage in between themselves. If a wife brings down a barrage of negative words on her husband, this can be very damaging to their relationship. Of course, men can dump verbally abusive language on their wives. Verbal abuse knows no gender restriction.

The use of many words is a source of power in a relationship. Women tend to use many more words in a day than most men do. On the contrary, men can be highly skilled in the use of words.

How many marriages have ended due to the misuse of words? It is well known that a thought can be communicated effectively or ineffectively by how well chosen the words are.

Power in a couple's relationship resides with this very use or disuse of words.

John Gottman* has shown that the number of positive versus negative exchanges a couple has when they are together impacts the toxicity of the relationship enormously. He says that there must be **at least five times as many positive versus negative interactions** for a marriage to be successful.

As a couple, it is very important for you to monitor the positive to negative ratio of comments you make to your significant other! Caustic comments are negative. Encouraging and affirming comments are positive. And repetition is important! You can't tell her/him you love her/him once and forget to say this again for a month.

People need to hear affirmation on a frequent basis. We don't tire of sincere positive comments. We become weary with negative ones. Positive comments from a person you love are especially important and meaningful.

Resource:
The Seven Principles for Making Marriage Work, John D. Gottman and Nan Silver, Crown Publishers.

Discussion Questions:
1. How do men relate positive thoughts to other men?

2. How do women relate positive thoughts to other women?

3. What are examples of positive versus negative words that couples give to each other?

4. How can you be more positive to each other?

Prayer Point/Take Away for Today:
I will say more positive than negative things to her/him.

Notes/Responses/Action:

-14-

SELF-IMAGE

Read: Genesis 1:27; Luke 6:45

Focus: God's plan for us is to build each other up.

Following up on positive versus negative words, how important are these comments to our image of ourselves? Except for narcissists, people often tend to put themselves down in conversation. We rarely applaud ourselves because it seems like self-conceit or self-aggrandizement. Since we don't speak well of ourselves for fear of being misunderstood, we often brush aside positive comments that come our way.

Negativity damages our self-image; hence, the five-to-one ratio of positive versus negative interactions recommended by Gottman.* This means that one of the most important things a couple can do to enhance their relationship is tell the truth about positive aspects of their partner's life and attitude. This means to be honest in our praise, not gushy or artificial.

People receive plenty of negativity, so a good dose of positive feedback rarely harms. Saying positive things helps offset negative experiences. And positive comments can insulate and heal us with respect to negative words from whatever the source.

If you were chewed out by your employer, the last thing you want to hear from your significant other is negative stuff when you are together. Positive words and actions within a relationship can build up a person's self-worth and offset much of what is inflicted by someone outside the relationship.

We each need to see ourselves as God sees us: "If God is for us, who can be against us?" (Romans 8:31b). You are a primary person who can bring God's love into focus for her/him.

Remember Genesis 1:27. Each of you is made in the image of God, and you are here for a purpose!

Resource:
The Seven Principles for Making Marriage Work, John D. Gottman and Nan Silver, Crown Publishers.

Discussion Questions:
1. Describe examples of someone who built up your self-image?

2. What are examples of positive things that can build up another person's self-image?

3. How can you tell if someone is insincere in trying to build up another person's self-image?

Prayer Point/Take Away for Today:
How can I build up her/his self-image in our relationship?

Notes/Responses/Action:

(Continued)

Notes/Responses/Action:

-15-

PERSONALITY

Read: Luke 6:37; Romans 14:12–13; 2 Peter 1:5–7

Focus: Accept each other for who you are.

Personality is an amazing combination of genetics and experiences. Studies of twins suggest that identical twins share about half of the same traits. On the other hand, fraternal twins share about 20 percent of the same traits.* Many studies indicate that much of our personality structure is fairly firmly fixed. So trying to drastically change another person in a dating or marriage relationship is not likely to have much positive effect. In fact, attempting to change someone can be downright irritating.

In addition, intentionally trying to change another person's personality traits is unwise. On the other hand, environmental modifications can take place related to many factors, such as age, maturity, continuity of roles, changes in family structures, etc.*

As humans, each of us has certain tendencies. Being aware of these may be helpful for premarried couples.

Many personality terms are part of our everyday vocabulary, such as introvert versus extrovert. If you are an outgoing person who loves to be with lots of people and your significant other is a homebody who is uncomfortable in crowds, don't expect much change as a result of forming a couple. Perhaps the best you can hope for is to follow a general concept which works much of the time: *Give the gift of your opposition.*

For the extrovert, this means that if you want to go out after working all day, say to your introverted significant other something like: "I want to go out with a bunch of friends. But because I love you, we can enjoy an evening by ourselves instead."

Of course, this allows the introvert to learn to say: "I'd really love to just be with you. But because you mean so much to me, let's go out and be with friends."

Give each other the gift of your opposite tendency. Be aware that the homebody will likely be exhausted after an intense group social event. And the outgoing person may feel a bit cramped when not with a group. If you use the opposition idea, don't keep track of whose turn it is!

Resource:
*https://www.verywellmind.com/are-personality-traits-caused-by-genes-or-environment-4120707

Discussion Questions:
1. Describe each other in terms of extrovert and introvert characteristics.

2. What are some ways you can give each other the "gift of your opposition"?

Prayer Point/Take Away for Today:
I will do something that she/he loves to do but I have difficulty enjoying.

Notes/Responses/Action:

(Continued)

Notes/Responses/Action:

-16-

INTERESTS: SIMILAR OR DIFFERENT?

Read: Proverbs 12:25

Focus: Kindness is never out of style.

This is a common phrase by many couples in the early stages of their relationship: "We have so much in common! This must be right!"

What does this really mean? Is it that you like the same sports? Or the same kinds of movies? Or the same fast food?

Let's return to the contrast between extroverts and introverts. Perhaps the most obvious contrast is how each likes to spend her/his free time. Introvert personalities tend to prefer to do things with a party of one or two, at the most. Their common leisure activities often include watching TV/movies, doing a hobby or craft, working in a shop or garden, repairing cars/house/appliances, reading, etc. An extrovert's preferred free time activities are spending time with groups of people, going out, and anything that involves interaction with more than a couple of individuals.

If you experience these contrasts, it is important to discuss such differences as premarrieds. It is usually wise to start to deal with differences before you say "I do" and start a life together.

Many people are not pure introverts or pure extroverts. This translates into enough variations to require discussion and understanding of contrasts and differences. Then find ways for each of you to respond to the other's interests.

Discussion Questions:
1. Discuss your personality differences in terms of interests.

2. Besides giving the "gift of your opposition," what other ways can you use to resolve or mute tensions related to personality?

3. What are some interests you could be involved in as a couple?

Prayer Point/Take Away for Today:
I'll ask if I can do something with her/him that I usually don't do.

Notes/Responses/Action:

(Continued)

Notes/Responses/Action:

-17-

HABITS: LIFE'S DETAILS

Read: Proverbs 11:11–13; Romans 12:2; Matthew 7:12

Focus: Be adaptable to his/her neutral habits.

Here's a bit of wisdom from a thoughtful person. We need habits so we can concentrate on the important things in life. That is probably true for individuals; however, habits can also place a strain on a couple's relationship.

Habits are largely learned. We began learning them as infants. Habits come in three styles: good, neutral, and bad.

Bad habits may be illegal, immoral, unhealthy, damaging to others or ourselves, and are often easily seen and identified by other people — whether or not we see them in ourselves. Good habits are just the opposite and may also be recognized by friends and relatives, and hopefully, ourselves.

The huge set of habits in the middle can provide most of the daily frustrations and tension in a relationship. To resolve these sorts of discomforts related to habit differences, it is important to have open and honest, but not angry, discussions.

Talking about habits during the dating stages can bring out potential stressors related to our habits. For example, I learned from my fiancée that doorknobs were not designed to be clothes hangers. That piece of knowledge saved some confrontations after we were married — maybe even on our wedding night! I discovered an amazing thing: I can change a habit!

On the good-bad habit spectrum, most habits are in the middle or neutral zone; they are neither good nor bad. Habits, since most are learned, can be modified, changed, dropped, or added to our repertoire of behaviors. There are a host of minute details in life that are not particularly life-threatening. So we may tend to let these irritations go, rather than discuss them in a calm and reasoned manner. But a direct discussion can gently relieve a pond full of frustrations and prevent the dam from breaking and allowing an overflow of emotion to cloud our relationship.

We are not talking about true obsessive-compulsive disorder (OCD), which is a condition of excessive or repetitive behavior that departs from simple habit. Such situations may require a therapist for help.

Entering into a marital relationship involves giving up some things and taking on others. Habits play an important part in this give-and-take process. You can't solve all habit issues before marriage, but honest discussions can set the tone for dealing with bothersome habits as they arise under a variety of conditions.

Now, while you're dating, is the time to talk about making some changes involving particularly irritating habits.

Discussion Questions:
1. Describe habits of your own that might be irritating to your significant other. For starters, how do you begin and end a day? Be specific.

2. Respond to the other's habits in terms of how accepting you are of their actions.

3. Describe how resistive you are about changing your habits.

4. Select one slightly annoying habit for each of you and discuss. Don't assume this habit will change. Do assume that you might become more accepting and less frustrated with the habit.

Prayer Point/Take Away for Today:
What habit might I change, for the sake of him/her?

Notes/Responses/Action:

(Continued)

Notes/Responses/Action:

-18-

VISITING A HOME

Read: Proverbs 25:19; 2 Timothy 1:5–7

Focus: Be sensitive to your significant other's background and family of origin.

We are all products of many influences in our lives up to this point. Not the least of these is the home we grew up in. There is a truism that counselors seem to agree on: *you do marry a family,* for good or ill. Couples often resist this statement but, on reflection, come to realize how much we are influenced by the home life we experienced.

One way to gain insight into your significant other is to visit the home where he/she grew up, if possible. Keep your eyes and ears open, but not in a detective sense.

After the visit, think about how your gender is a part of the family structure. Are there clues that might suggest gender repression or lack of equality? Is anyone a doormat in the family? How are household chores handled? What is the family conversation like around a dinner table? Or do they even eat together? Would you want to be treated the way your gender (or position in family) is treated in that home?

A discussion following visits to your respective homes could be very helpful in deciding what each of you wants to keep from your home background and what you want to leave behind.

Too often, this sort of candor is missing in a premarital discussion, except in the presence of a pastor or counselor.

There will very likely need to be changes on the part of both you and your partner. Accepting this fact can go a long way toward eventually developing a happy married life. After all, you will be establishing a new family unit and culture. Now is the time to begin thinking about what you want it to look like.

Discussion Questions:
1. Describe the family environment each of you brings to your relationship.

2. What do you think you would like to keep, modify, or delete from your family backgrounds in the relationship you might form as a couple?

3. Discuss what might be unique in your future family (if you decide to marry).

Prayer Point/Take Away for Today:
What might she/he think after a visit to my home?

Notes/Responses/Action:

(Continued)

Notes/Responses/Action:

-19-

MESSIES VERSUS CLEANIES

Read: Proverbs 15:33

Focus: When faced with differences, first be wise.

No one needs to define a *messie* or a *cleanie*; the words are self-explanatory. The differences are clear. It is also not a surprise that cleanies and messies often marry each other.

These patterns are partly learned but may grow out of certain personality types. There are lots of websites dealing with messies but very few on cleanies! Sandra Fenton* describes some of the reasons behind messiness. She says messies often have high ideals, are well-educated and successful, with big ideas and ambition. This may grow out of perfectionism and can produce: a lack of focus, fear of losing control, not having enough to help others, a desire to do only big jobs and avoid small ones, sentimentality about throwing things out, and being visually tuned out to the local environment.

On the other side of the story, Fenton says cleanies express perfectionistic tendencies by needing order in their lives and environment. Often, this is a characteristic from childhood when order was rewarded. Psychologists separate perfectionism from OCD, which is more extreme in its behavioral manifestations.

Cleanies often clash with messies wherever there is a lack of cleanliness in a home or other living environment. They may argue about how organized a room is (e.g., folded clothes, stacked magazines, etc.), and about anything related to planning or carrying out a plan.

Here is a list of suggested coping mechanisms for married messie/cleanie couples to live together in reasonable harmony. **

- Learn how to communicate and negotiate without insulting or cutting down your partner.

- Do not accuse, but ask to work on the problem.

- Set up messie and cleanie zones.

- Use your smartphone to set times for a project to be completed.

- Talk about why each is concerned or not concerned with an issue.

- There may be something in a person's background driving a particular behavior or concern.

- Don't take the differences personally. The situation may have nothing to do with you.

- If you can afford it, hire someone to clean the house or apartment, if that will help.

- Remember why you are together: you love each other.

Resources:
*www.imom.com/6-reasons-why-the-messie-is-messy/#.W-dJyeJRfcs
**www.today.com/health/study-reveals-how-neat-freak-slob-can-live-peace-924727

Discussion Questions:
1. Take turns describing yourselves on the messie-cleanie spectrum.

2. What messie/cleanie issues have you experienced in the past and how were these resolved, if they were resolved?

3. Discuss ways you could resolve messie-cleanie issues if you decide to marry.

Prayer Point/Take Away for Today:
Am I a messie or cleanie? Should I change my behavior?

Notes/Responses/Action:

(Continued)

Notes/Responses/Action:

-20-

WORDS: THE STUFF OF COMMUNICATION

Read: Psalm 19:14; Proverbs 16:24, 18:20, 20:15, 27:9

Focus: Choose your words wisely!

Words are the most important tools in your relationship toolbox. What you say and how you say it are key to developing a happy and fulfilling relationship. Using language to build connections pays big dividends.

Effective communication is not, contrary to popular thought, rocket science. Innumerable books have been written on how women and men communicate differently.* Boiling things down to the bare minimum, two things stand up and shout about how to communicate well: **Listen to understand** and **speak with the other person in mind.**

Speaking with the other person in mind means to be aware of what someone else may hear and how they may understand what we are saying. It is one thing to say something, but quite another to try to say it from the other person's point of view. Ask yourself: "How will she/he take what I say?" This single approach can save the great percentage of misunderstandings and hurt feelings between couples.

Doing this properly does take some thought; but if you know something about the other person, you can craft your words so you are clear and aware how your words may be interpreted or misinterpreted. If you think your words will create anger, hurt, discouragement, or other negative feelings, you have the ability to adjust how and what you will say. Perhaps we should say nothing! Sometimes, we should do what only humans can do: **wait before reacting, and then decide what to say, if anything.**

The other big part of effective communication is listening well. This can be a chore for some, especially males. As an exercise, eavesdrop on a group of women talking. Then listen in as a group of men talk. Notice the difference? Generally, the women listen carefully and respond sympathetically to each other, unless somebody is mad at somebody else! The men may offer advice, whether asked for it or not, but are more likely waiting to jump into the conversation with a bigger or more powerful story than the previous speaker. These are quite generalized but not uncommon differences in genders.*

Men can learn a great deal by observing how a woman listens to another woman.* Notice that there is usually very clear eye contact between the women. Also, there are frequent reinforcing verbals: "Yes," "Really?", "My!", etc. Most men can improve their conversations with women by maintaining eye contact and letting her know you are still awake! Here's a hint from a famous speaker. Rather than staring into both her eyes, focus on her left eye. This apparently affects the right side of her brain (hocus-pocus maybe, but it seems to work and prevents her from becoming uncomfortable).

If your conversations often end with frustration, try the above two approaches and note if things turn out better. Seeing things from the other person's point of view and paying attention as he/she speaks are gold when it comes to building a couple's relationship.

Resources:
You Just Don't Understand, Deborah Tannen, Ballantine Books.
Men are from Mars, Women are from Venus, John Gray, HarperCollins Publishers.
The Seven Principles for Making Marriage Work, John M. Gottman and Nan Silver, Crown Publishers.

Discussion Questions:
1. How would you describe your word communication with each other? Take turns illustrating what speaks most effectively to you.

2. This week, do your best to speak with your significant other's understanding in mind.

3. If you have difficulty concentrating on what she/he is saying, try the left eye approach.

Prayer Point/Take Away for Today:
I will do better at paying attention to what he/she is saying.

Notes/Responses/Action:

(Continued)

Notes/Responses/Action:

WORDS: BUILD UP OR BREAK DOWN

Read: Matthew 7:3–4; 1 Peter 4:8

Focus: Say the good word.

Our words have huge power. They can build a relationship, or they can destroy it. Think of a TV drama or movie where you saw this happening. What approach destroyed the relationship? Or what resolved the problem and built up the relationship?

A careful analysis usually reveals some obvious mistakes or successes. Criticism and cynical words did not help. Flashes of anger and hotly spoken words that fried the other person were effective only for destroying the relationship.

On the other hand, admission of guilt or responsibility and requests for forgiveness usually were healing. Kind, thoughtful words blunted emotional outbursts and drew the persons together.

Simple solutions would have transformed negative experiences into positive ones. That is why **thinking before speaking** is so important. Some suggest counting to three before responding to a negative or irritating comment. Use your unique human ability to give some thought to what you might say.

Irrational bursts of emotion-filled angry words do nothing but defeat any attempt at solving a problem. But thoughtful, calm words tend to reduce the emotion of the moment and foster better understanding.*

Resource:
Why Marriages Succeed or Fail, John Gottman with Nan Silver, Fireside, Simon and Schuster.

Discussion Questions:
1. Describe successful and unsuccessful communication you have experienced with each other.

2. How did you bring about resolution of the issue? If the problem was not resolved, what might be done to achieve a better outcome?

3. What might you do to improve your use of words with each other? Share what words are especially important for you to hear.

Prayer Point/Take Away for Today:
What words can I use that will encourage him/her?

Notes/Responses/Action:

(Continued)

Notes/Responses/Action:

-22-

WORDS: FIX OR LISTEN

Read: Proverbs 18:13

Focus: Think before you answer an unasked question.

One of the most frustrating conversational methods that almost never works is to try and *fix* the other person's problem — unless a *repair* is requested. If someone is telling you about a problem, the *answer* or solution may be obvious to you. So the natural tendency is to break in and offer how you think she/he should solve the problem.

If that has happened to you, it is no surprise that this was likely upsetting — especially if you hadn't finished telling your story!

Many people don't want your opinion about how to fix their problem. This may seem strange to you as a listener. Often they just want to describe the issue and enlist your ability to listen to them. Often, the truth is that they can solve their own problems; they just need an audience to listen to their frustration.

Many of us like to wear the Mr./Ms. Fixit hat.* Why? Because, in our unfathomable wisdom, we can resolve things quickly and move on to the next subject. Here is the clue. The other person may only want you to put on your Listening Cap and keep your solutions to yourself!

All this is set aside if the person actually *requests* your opinion. Then you are free to carefully, and without seeming to be a know-it-all, discuss your thoughts on the subject. You might be a real help in the process. If you are the one who wants to tell your story of frustration, you might say to your eager fix-it person that you just need a kind and attentive ear.

Resource:
*https://www.familiesonlinemagazine.com/couples/mr-fix-it.html

Discussion Questions:
1. How do you feel when someone breaks into your story with a fix-it approach? Share examples.

2. What can you do if you feel that you know the answer to someone's problem, but they don't ask for your opinion?

Prayer Point/Take Away for Today:
I will avoid trying to fix her/him.

Notes/Responses/Action:

(Continued)

Notes/Responses/Action:

-23-

WORDS: NAGGING AND TELLING THE TRUTH

Read: Proverbs 21:9

Focus: No one likes to be nagged!

No one likes a nagger, someone who always seems to be harping on one flaw or another that we may or may not know we have. Nagging may be funny in a TV program, but it is no fun in real life.

What is the problem with nagging? The universal response I have heard is: "It is irritating!"

Why does nagging bother us? Nagging usually focuses on some weakness that the nagger feels the need to address. Nagging is never requested, but it is spoken anyway! Naggers have the problem solved and want you to fix yourself or have you find someone who can help you. Unfortunately, naggers often don't think they are nagging; they are simply offering an observation, and perhaps how you might use their observation of your behavior to shape up!

There is one underlying thought to consider if you feel that someone is nagging you. Perhaps there might be a seed of truth in the nag. That doesn't justify nagging. But it might pay to consider the nagger's words before writing them off completely.

The problem with nagging is that you may know there is some truth in what they say, but you are offended by the nagger's approach. Their continual reminders really bug you. Nagging rarely works and often prevents a person from making any changes that a nagger suggests. If told they are nagging, the offender doesn't usually see it that way. After all, they believe that somebody needed to say there is a problem!

Then there is the person who likes to "tell the whole truth." This may seem like a good thing, but such an approach ends up sounding a lot like nagging. Telling the whole truth is a misnomer and is usually just another excuse to nag.

Nagging does not build a relationship. Being honest in a relationship usually means telling the truth gently. Your tone of voice can make a big difference as to the outcome when you tell the truth. Remember that people love a good listener. They never appreciate a nagger.

Discussion Questions:
1. Do a self-inspection. Have you nagged recently? If so, why? Share examples.

2. If you have felt nagged, how did it make you feel? Share examples.

3. What is a better way to communicate than by nagging?

Prayer Point/Take Away for Today:
I will think before saying something that might sound like nagging.

Notes/Responses/Action:

(Continued)

Notes/Responses/Action:

-24-
WORDS: EXPRESSING A NEED

Read: Proverbs 8:6–9

Focus: Be clear and accurate.

One of the more difficult pieces of communication is how to express a need without seeming to be selfish. Narcissism is a disorder that focuses on the self to an extreme. For a narcissist, the world revolves around her/him. So, if we have a specific need in a relationship, the last thing we want to do is appear to have this disorder.

Yet, your needs are real, and your significant other may not know what you need without hearing that from you. This is where it gets delicate. Words become very important when you express a need. Avoid any hint of selfishness; that would be counterproductive.

One approach is to express your needs in terms of building your relationship. This tends to blunt a misinterpretation that you are being purely selfish. Expressing a need in a relationship is very important for both parties. Your goal is to understand each other and meet each other's needs. A dating or marriage relationship is a two-way street with both receiving benefits. The overall result should strengthen the bond you feel.

It is important to ask the other person about their needs that are not being met. You can foster an atmosphere of mutual expression of needs by asking good questions. If neither knows what the other needs, then frustration and unhappiness can result. Say your need, clearly and with humility but never as an accusation. Listen to the other person's expression of needs without judging or rejecting.

Discussion Questions:
1. What ways of expressing a need would be counterproductive?

2. Discuss an example of a need that each of you may have and which the other could meet in terms of building your relationship.

Prayer Point/Take Away for Today:
I will express any need I have in a careful manner that is still honest. I will listen to her/his expression of needs with compassion and love.

Notes/Responses/Action:

(Continued)

Notes/Responses/Action:

-25-
WORDS: COMMUNICATING FEELINGS

Read: Proverbs 17:27

Focus: Say how you feel but with care.

Many studies* indicate that not everyone talks about their feelings as well as others do. Women are often more effective in their emotional language than many men are.

To improve a man's ability to speak about his feelings, a woman may need to demonstrate by using words which convey how she feels. The object is not to make men into women. That would be a very bad thing! Instead, men can learn to understand the feeling language used by women and speak their own feelings better.

If a person is bottled up inside and can't express what is going on, then communication with a significant other is limited. Being able to describe the stresses of life verbally can be very freeing and can allow healing to take place.

Men rarely speak feelings within their gender group, but can learn to talk openly with their significant other. This is a private matter and is one of the beautiful things about male-female communication. The use of words to convey the stresses we sense can allow a couple to have a communication line that is unique and very affirming for their relationship. Take advantage of feeling language and practice using it.

Resource:
*https://psychcentral.com/blog/6-ways-men-and-women-communicate-differently/

Discussion Questions:
1. Talk about the use of feeling words in your conversations. Give examples.

2. What are ways to express stresses in words?

3. What are ways to express happiness in words?

4. How should you respond to your significant other's feeling words?

Prayer Point/Take Away for Today:
I will listen for feeling words in her/his speech and respond appropriately. I will use feeling words in my speech.

Notes/Responses/Action:

(Continued)

Notes/Responses/Action:

-26-

WORDS: HUMOR

Read: Proverbs 17:22

Focus: Good humor is healthy!

God gifts human beings with an amazing quality: humor. Laughter and amusement are second nature to us. Studies* suggest that humor is a factor in couple attraction.

Laughing — not just smiling, but real belly laughs — provides huge health benefits.** One well known individual, when he received the news of his serious illness, found all the funny movies he could and watched them. Apparently, he laughed himself back to health! This is not to indicate that we should avoid physicians and hire comedians!

I have been told many times by women that one of the important attractions that drew them to their significant other was: "He makes me laugh." Why is laughing so good for couples? Perhaps there is bonding as a result of this basic human characteristic. Whatever the reason, please laugh a lot!

But in a family, humor has its limits. We must avoid the sarcastic laughter involved when one of the family members is continually picked on in a derogatory manner. Perhaps all families have some in-house humor that comes out of a shared experience. No one else might see the humor or maybe it is so private that it is not shared outside the family.

One married couple learned this lesson well as a result of a kitchen disaster. One was at work, and the other ended up with a kitchen filled with burned food. On reciting the tale, the victim of the catastrophe was anything but in good humor. The spouse nodded with understanding and did not smile. After reciting the problem, the person saw the humor in the story and laughed. The listener could then laugh, too. The rule:Don't laugh too soon! So, feel free to laugh out loud! It does a body good!

Resources:
*https://news.ku.edu/2015/08/27/first-comes-laughter-then-love-study-finds-out-why-humor-important-romantic-attraction
**https://www.helpguide.org/articles/mental-health/laughter-is-the-best-medicine.htm

Discussion Questions:

1. Take turns describing your ability to laugh.

2. What kind of humor do you enjoy most?

3. Tell a funny story about yourself.

Prayer Point/Take Away for Today:
I will laugh at something I have done. I will avoid laughing at others to make fun of them.

Notes/Responses/Action:

(Continued)

Notes/Responses/Action:

WE ARE ALL A LITTLE WEIRD

Read: Proverbs 27:6

Focus: Accept wise counsel, even when it hurts.

Everybody has quirks. A big key to a happy relationship is to learn to accept each other, quirks and all. Nobody is perfect — just in case you were uncertain! Yet, our perfectionistic tendencies trick us into thinking that our partner should be perfect. Of course, they are not. What do we do when we learn this important fact (and this probably happens in the second or third stage of dating)?

Perhaps the best thing to do is admit your own faults and learn to accept the faults of your significant other. Who can you change? Not her/him! The best you can do is accept who you are and accept who she/he is.

No use fooling yourself into trying to fix any of his/her weirdnesses. Just work on your own and see if that triggers a similar response in the other person. Acceptance is a wonderful virtue in a couple's relationship. Know that many things will never change, so get over trying to twist her/him into your mold. Accept him/her as he/she is and grow yourself, with God's help.

This caveat should not be ignored: can you live with the imperfections of him/her? Can he/she live with yours? Is this a clue that the relationship needs to mature or to break up? Be honest with yourself and him/her.

Discussion Questions:

1. Take turns describing some of your own goofy quirks. Laugh together.

2. Talk about ways to accept each other and let God work on each of you.

Prayer Point/Take Away for Today:
I will be more accepting of her/his uniquenesses.

Notes/Responses/Action:

(Continued)

Notes/Responses/Action:

-28-

LOVE LANGUAGE

Read: Proverbs 12:22; Colossians 3:14

Focus: Nothing beats love.

Gary Chapman* has probably done more to assist couples in understanding their differences and how to relate to each other than anyone can imagine. He discovered that everyone has a primary way that they understand and receive love. He calls this your *love language*. The five ways we recognize love are:

- words of affirmation
- quality time
- receiving gifts
- acts of service
- physical touch

He also indicates that we have a secondary love language, and a third, etc. But one of these five ways is the primary way we really recognize as someone expressing love to us.

If your significant other most enjoys spending quality time with you, then that is her/his primary love language. But if your personal love language is physical touch, then you may not understand her/his spending quality time with you as love. Another example might be where one person loves to receive gifts, but their companion recognizes words of affirmation as the big deal. They each understand a significant love event only when the activity fits their personal love language.

In order to express love to someone, it is important to do something that fits the language of love that is *primary* for them. When your special person goes out of her/his way to express love in your love language, you know it! The point is: different people have different love languages. When we learn someone's primary love language and behave toward them in that manner, then they feel loved.

The problem arises when we try to express our love language to someone who has a different love language. For example, suppose receiving gifts is your primary love language, but your spouse needs quality time as her/his primary love language in order to feel loved. If you give him/her a gift, he/she may acknowledge the gift but with little satisfaction. You may feel hurt that the gift was not well-received. Both of you feel less than happy as a result of not interacting with the appropriate love language.

Figuring out one's love language is not difficult. Go online to take an assessment or just make observations or talk about it together. Then focus on giving your special person what they recognize as their primary love language. Both can be happy with the result.

I encourage both of you to read this very helpful book by Gary Chapman. BTW: Reading a book together can open the door to great couple discussion starters.

Note: Physical touch, as a love language, does not necessarily mean sex. You have probably known individuals who seem unable to speak without touching you. Physical touch is likely their love language.

Resource:
The Five Love Languages, Gary Chapman, Northfield Publishing.

Discussion Questions:
1. What do you think are the primary love languages of your parents?

2. Evaluate each of your love language(s).

3. Discuss how each of you can express the other's love language.

Prayer Points/Take Away for Today:
How can I express my love based on her/his love language?

Notes/Responses/Action:

(Continued)

Notes/Responses/Action:

-29-

APOLOGY LANGUAGE

Read: Colossians 3:13

Focus: Forgiveness is essential.

Because we are human, we make mistakes and need to give someone an apology. Gary Chapman teamed with Jennifer Thomas* to discover the ways in which we recognize an apology. As with the five love languages, we understand an apology when it is couched in the appropriate language of apology. The five apology languages are:

1. Expressing regret: "I'm sorry."

2. Accepting responsibility: "Know what, I was just plain wrong."

3. Making restitution: "I'd like to make this right between us. What can I do?"

4. Genuinely repenting: "That is something I don't want to do again."

5. Requesting forgiveness: "Can you forgive me, please?"

Note that the languages range from a fairly low level of regret to a high level of sorrow. The exact words to use are not significant, but the idea needs to be expressed.

Since everyone understands apology in their own way, it is important to learn to express an apology in a manner that your significant other understands. Number one may not even be considered an apology for many people. They need to hear something at a higher level in the hierarchy of apology to understand that an apology is your intent.

Resource:
The Five Languages of Apology, Gary Chapman and Jennifer Thomas, Northfield Publishing.

Discussion Questions:
1. Take turns describing what each of you considers as an apology. Does the level of apology depend on the infraction? If so, how?

2. How have you apologized to each other in the past? How might you need to change in the future?

Prayer Point/Take Away for Today:
When I goof up, I will do my best to apologize using her/his apology language.

Notes/Responses/Action:

(Continued)

Notes/Responses/Action:

-30-

WHEN YOU ARE WRONG

Read: James 5:16a

Focus: Confession heals.

Since each of you understands apologies in a different way, it is important to recognize when you make an error and that you know how to make amends. Others see our actions and words from their perspective. We see them from our own bias.

Typically, we try to justify what we do and say by playing the *blame game*. This is easily done by throwing responsibility onto someone else: our significant other, a family member, our work environment, how we feel, sickness, the government, the church — you name it, and somebody besides me is the cause! This immature approach never solves the problem. Only when we sing the old song, "It's me, it's me, it's me, O Lord, standin' in the need of prayer" can we start to rebuild a broken or cracked relationship.

We are responsible for what we say and what we do. Oh, there are outside influences to be sure, but the decisions we make and actions we take are our responsibility. God has given us a totally unique ability, among all the millions of species on Earth: we can choose what we will do! Theologians call this *free will*. This powerful gift, combined with faith and prayer, can allow us to "move mountains," as Jesus said.

When we try to blame others, we shirk our ability to own what we do. And we mute the value of God's gift of choice. Breaking the cycle of throwing our bad behavior and words on others frees us from our natural tendencies and builds bridges to connect us with people we care about.

The bottom line is to admit when you are wrong, apologize, and move forward in your relationship. Confession opens the door for acceptance and healing.

Discussion Questions:

1. Why is it so difficult to admit when we are wrong? Share examples.

2. When someone admits being wrong, how should you respond?

3. Describe a time when you admitted being wrong and what helped resolve the issue.

Prayer Point/Take Away for Today:

I will do my best to admit being wrong sooner than I usually do.

Notes/Responses/Action:

(Continued)

Notes/Responses/Action:

-31-

ANGER

Read: James 1:19–20; Psalm 19:14, 37:8; Ecclesiastes 7:9; Proverbs 14:29, 15:1, 15:18, 19:11, 22:24, 29:11; Ephesians 4:26; Colossians 3:8

Focus: Anger usually gets you nowhere that you want to go.

We are emotional beings. God gave us the ability to choose how to react when faced with danger. You have probably heard of *flight* or *fight* as the response choices we can make in a dangerous situation. That is the case for most organisms, but there is another approach: *cooperation*. Jesus taught His followers that when faced with an adversary, they should take this third approach.

How might cooperation look in a situation where a couple faces off and anger reaches the danger point of harming the relationship? First of all, remember that anger is not, in itself, evil. "Be angry and sin not" (Ephesians 4:26). Jesus displayed anger when He drove out money changers from the Temple. So, anger is not the issue.

What we do with the anger is what is important*. In the book of Proverbs, there is a significant statement: "A soft answer turns away wrath" (Proverbs 15:1). Many who try this approach find that it keeps disagreements from becoming destructive arguments. One author suggests that stretching your fingers, when you sense you are clinching your fists, also helps.

Probably the most important thing is to stop talking and analyze what you are doing. Pushing ahead when angry rarely resolves the issue. Another source recommends asking for a pause, then returning to the discussion later — perhaps in an hour, if possible.

Your posture is important in dealing with an emotionally charged topic. Sit side by side instead of facing each other. When you are beside someone and touching them, focusing on the problem in front of you — as opposed to thinking that the other is the problem — is much easier. And always avoid those antagonizing "you" statements ("You always ___" and "You never ___"). Instead, use "I" statements ("When this happens, I feel ___"). And above all, remember what you want to happen, which is to build a loving relationship that remains strong even when you disagree.

Note: If there are serious anger issues, it might be best to seek help from a counselor or therapist.

Resource:
*https://www.mayoclinic.org/healthy-lifestyle/adult-health/in-depth/anger-management/art-20045434

Discussion Questions:
1. Describe a recent heated discussion or argument you had with each other (BTW: They do happen, so don't be surprised!). How did you resolve the issue? Or how might it be resolved now?

2. Describe a better way of resolving concerns each of you has. Or, if you resolved an argument so both were happy with the result, how can you repeat the method?

Prayer Point/Take Away for Today:
If I feel anger rising during a discussion with her/him, I will pause and think and breath a prayer.

Notes/Responses/Action:

-32-

JEALOUSY

Read: Proverbs 27:4, 14:30; 1 Corinthians 3:3;
2 Corinthians 12:20; Galatians 5:19–20

Focus: The book of Proverbs presents an Old Testament description of the contrasting emotions by comparing a thief to an adulter (Proverbs 6:30–35). The Jewish "eye for an eye" takes it even further, which illustrates the power of jealousy. In the New Testament, St. Paul's notes on jealousy classify it with some awful sins.

Jealousy in a relationship is an emotional powerhouse that can destroy the beautiful picture of marital happiness found throughout the Bible. There is a good form of jealousy and also a bad form.* The good form involves commitment and protection of your relationship. The bad form is quite different and often involves feelings of inadequacy and unresolved issues.

Common causes that trigger the bad form of jealousy frequently revolve around real or imagined romantic connections between someone outside the relationship and the other person in the relationship. To avoid this sort of trigger, both partners need to be discrete when interacting with another member of the opposite gender. Friendships are fine, but the stage is set for misinterpretation and jealous feelings when a partner crosses certain lines.

Once a partner crosses those lines, restoring a couple's equilibrium can be difficult. Often, there was no intentional bad behavior, but she/he made inappropriate choices. It is often difficult to explain this away. Better to be safe than sorry. In many cases, a third party counselor/pastor may be needed to help restore the relationship.

There is also the jealousy that comes when one partner is too consumed with work, sports, digital entertainment, volunteer service, church activities, etc. Open, honest discussions need to occur so the offended partner can voice her/his concerns. The jealousy here is usually not as intense as sexually related jealousy, but the loneliness and disrespect created by too much outside commitment still hurts. This can provide a temptation to seek friendships outside the marriage that may turn into unfaithfulness. If this happens, a married couple should seek counseling, and the outside contact needs to end.

The bottom line is to avoid the triggers that generate jealous feelings. If one partner is too possessive, then jealousy can lurk at the door, ready to disrupt an otherwise good relationship. Possessiveness may indicate other problem issues, such as prior relationships with persons who cheated. Again, outside help from a pastor or counselor is wise, especially if the problem escalates.

Talking about your outside relationships and other commitments can cut off the triggers before they become a problem. Everyone wants to be in a relationship with someone who is faithful. Avoid the appearance of wrong behavior (1 Thessalonians 5:22).

Although the above discussion seems focused on marital jealousy, similar situations can arise with couples who are not married but are in a serious dating or engaged relationship. The principles involved are similar, and so are the solutions.

Resource:
*https://www.focusonthefamily.ca/content/understanding-healthy-and-unhealthy-jealousy

Discussion Questions:

Note: If there are sensitive issues here, consider doing this in the presence of a counselor/pastor.

1. If appropriate, discuss any concerns related to outside influences, regardless of the type.

2. How difficult would it be for you to forgive someone who is unfaithful?

3. What would be needed for you to forgive an unfaithful person? Where does the grace of God enter for you?

Prayer Point/Take Away for Today:
Am I doing something that could create a jealousy problem for him/her in our relationship?

Notes/Responses/Action:

(Continued)

Notes/Responses/Action:

-33-

CONFLICT RESOLUTION

Read: James 1:19; Psalm 19:14; Proverbs 12:18, 18:13;
Ephesians 4:29; Philippians 2:4; Colossians 3:13; 1 Peter 3:8–9

Focus: Resolving a conflict involves listening a lot and speaking less.

Resolving conflict is perhaps one of the most important skills that a couple can learn. Unfortunately, most couples enter marriage without training in this key area. Yet, the training is not high order learning! And learning to deal with conflict in a relationship is fundamental to keeping equilibrium in marriage.

The first thing to be very clear about is that you will have conflicts! Some people, when viewing a couple from the outside, might say, "Oh, they never argue. They are the perfect couple." Maybe not in public, but virtually all couples have issues over which they may become quite emotional. So, expect conflicts to arise. The reality is that you both have opinions. Differences of opinion are normal in a marital relationship and can help a couple avoid mistakes. Those differences can also fuel conflict.

Once you recognize the seed that can germinate into a conflict, kick into conflict-resolving mode. Otherwise, the emotional nature of a disagreement can cause feelings to escalate and reach unhealthy levels.

Either one or both of you may realize that an issue is causing feelings to rise in temperature and should call for a pause in the discussion. Whoever recognizes this can start to turn down the heat by asking the basic question: "What are we arguing about?" It is very important for both of you to be on the same page. Sometimes you are each talking about something different! Agree on what the issue is. Then talk about the perspective each of you brings to the discussion. How have you handled it in the past? What is the best way to handle it now?

If you are both stumped about how to proceed or have difficulty seeing each other's views, agree to stop and start over from scratch. On a piece of paper, create a list of things you might do to solve or resolve whatever you are talking about. Together, choose a likely scenario and agree to work on this approach.

Become collaborators to attack the problem rather than attackers of each other. After you have tried your part, return and discuss the results. Give high-fives for success or choose another solution to try.

Usually, something like the above approach* can bring the emotional responses down and let your rational minds take over. The goal is to strengthen, not weaken, your relationship.

Resource:
*https://www.amanet.org/training/articles/the-five-steps-to-conflict-resolution.aspx

Discussion Questions:
1. Talk about a conflict that you have had. How was it resolved, or was it resolved?

2. What might you do to resolve conflicts in the future?

3. How do you feel after resolving a conflict?

Prayer Point/Take Away for Today:

The next time we have a conflict, I will pause and ask why we are arguing.

Notes/Responses/Action:

(Continued)

Notes/Responses/Action:

-34-

EATING

Read: Proverbs 23:6; 1 Corinthians 10:31

Focus: Let food be a calming influence.

Of all the things that people do together, eating is a common denominator. In very early times, families ate almost every meal together. Now, the rush of modern life makes eating three meals a day in each other's presence an impossible dream.

Food has the potential to bond people. Technology can be a distraction during a meal, since this is one of the few times when everyone can speak to the family group. Eating together provides an ideal time to discuss what each has done during the day, to share ideas, to ask and answer questions, and generally to see where everyone is in their lives.

Too often, the meal table has been used as a time for delivering discipline or chastising particular family members. Michael Hyatt* lists ways of making a meal together into a positive experience. Here are a few of his suggestions.

1. Ask open-ended questions, like:

- What is your favorite music, best movie, etc., and why?

- What do you like most about (name a person in the family)?

- If running for President, what promise would you work to keep?

2. Involve everyone in the conversation by asking, "What do you think?"

3. Do more listening than talking.

4 Affirm people, even if you disagree with them.

The point is to keep the conversation from focusing on negative ideas and criticism of people. Involve everyone and focus on a positive attitude to help make mealtime enjoyable.

Resource:
*michaelhyatt.com/how-to-have-better-dinner-conversations

Discussion Questions:
1. What were mealtimes like for you growing up?

2. What would you like to retain, drop, or modify from your family-of-origin mealtimes?

3. What can you do to make eating together more pleasant and meaningful?

4. How can cell phones/technology devices be dealt with to encourage face-to-face communication during family meals?

Prayer Point/Take Away for Today:
When we eat together, I will give you my full attention and keep the conversation going.

Notes/Responses/Action:

(Continued)

Notes/Responses/Action:

-35-

FOOD CULTURE

Read: Proverbs 31:14

Focus: Food comes from many sources.

In developing countries, gathering food is often a daily event. Since there may be no way of preserving food, people either buy food from a market or find it. With the availability of frozen and canned goods and refrigeration plus a well-organized delivery system, we gather food less frequently. In more developed countries, many different types of food are available, which allows for the evolution of a variety of tastes and preferences.

Merging a woman and a man from two different food cultures can create an interesting and potentially challenging situation. Food cultures vary not only from country to country, but also between families.

One of the most helpful exercises a premarried couple can do to deal with these differences involves a visit to a local supermarket. Together, they walk all the aisles and symbolically "buy" food and other products, pretending they are preparing for a week's worth of meals. This can bring out such subtleties as which brand name to purchase, as well as larger food preferences. For a bigger challenge, tabulate the costs involved. After you have finished, save this information so you can use it to help build a budget.

Discussion Questions:
1. Visit a supermarket and choose what you would buy if purchasing food for a week. Take time to discuss each other's preferences.

2. After this activity, evaluate how you might adapt to each other's food choices.

Prayer Point/Take Away for Today:
I will try one new food that she/he enjoys.

Notes/Responses/Action:

(Continued)

Notes/Responses/Action:

-36-

FOOD PREPARATION

Read: Genesis 1:29

Focus: There are many types of foods. Who prepares food?

With the huge availability of already prepared food, many persons grow up without significant kitchen skills. Rapid-paced living subsidizes supermarkets, and fast food restaurants require only a credit card to have a tempting meal delivered to your home.

It is well documented that food prepared in restaurants is, by and large, less nutritious and less healthy than meals prepared at home. Eating out may be fun, but avoiding the kitchen can have long-term effects, both for health and for family bonding. A couple just married can often not afford to spend money on pre-prepared food. Certainly, eating out on occasion can be helpful, especially when both are worn out from work. But this is not a healthy habit.

The important point here is to work together in the home. This may take a wide variety of forms. Some couples take turns or share food preparation responsibilities. Others designate one as the main chef, and the other has clean-up duty. Some specialize in shopping for food.

The possibilities are many. Enjoy the pleasure of shared responsibilities related to food.

Discussion Questions:
1. What was it like in your home concerning food shopping, preparation, serving, or clean up? How were you involved?

2. How might you see yourself and your significant other in the food preparation arena?

Prayer Point/Take Away for Today:
I will think about my involvement in food preparation in my future home.

Notes/Responses/Action:

(Continued)

Notes/Responses/Action:

-37-

EDUCATION

Read: Acts 7:22; Proverbs 23:12

Focus: Education can affect relationships.

In a world where education of large populations is a widespread goal, the diversity of academic backgrounds is very great. For many previous generations, a college education was a rarity. With many persons attaining bachelor, master, and doctoral degrees, the spread of educational attainments for couples can range from slight to significant.

It is not surprising that many couples meet while studying at similar educational levels. Because many persons become attracted to those they grew up near, some couples' educational backgrounds may range from high school graduates to graduate-level degrees. No matter the educational level differences, there are many more significant factors that contribute to a happy marriage.

Sometimes, the contrast in educational levels does show up in areas that require attention. For example, there may be large differences in musical appreciation, reading preferences, theatrical awareness, sports interests, and artistic tastes. How a couple deals with such contrasts can be critical. Acceptance of dissimilarities is important.

Working out how partners spend their free time based on educational backgrounds is not insignificant. Neither partner should feel disenfranchised because of these differences. Don't let education negatively affect your relationship. Embrace the uniqueness of backgrounds that each of you might bring to your potential marriage.

Discussion Questions:
1. Discuss your educational backgrounds, what or who influenced you educationally, and how you feel about your education.

2. How does your educational background affect what you like to do for fun?

3. Do you have additional educational goals? If so, how might these be achieved, if you marry?

Prayer Point/Take Away for Today:
I will do my best to relate to her/his educational background and goals in a positive manner.

Notes/Responses/Action:

(Continued)

Notes/Responses/Action:

-38-

LEISURE

Read: Exodus 33:14; Ephesians 5:15–16

Focus: Leisure is necessary but must be measured.

Regardless of how busy we are, there is always at least some free time — time not required by work, school, home, relatives, friends, or other commitments. The world has innumerable ways of occupying your free time. What are your favorite things to do when you are not required to be somewhere or do something?

You and your significant other each have preferences of how to spend your time when there is nothing else to do. How well do your preferences match?

A well-balanced couple should not be joined at the hip. There should be both shared interests and separate interests. These can take many forms. The entertainment industry has created a diverse set of activities, many of which can be done together and many singularly. Here are a few examples.

1. TV, theater, and movies: What genre(s) do you prefer? How is the remote controlled?

2. Sports: Spectator, participant, or both?

3. Games: Table and board, cards, video/online games

4. Outdoor: Hiking, running, bird watching, flying, biking, nature photography

5. Collecting: Gathering objects of personal interest

6. Creativity and hobbies: Crafts, art, music, building, writing, repairing, remodeling, landscaping, inventing, experimenting

7. Reading: Which genre(s)?

Certain personality types often choose certain ways to use leisure time. Highly organized individuals may have specific times, places, and situations preset in their smartphones. On the other hand, spontaneous individuals are more prone to quick changes and decisions. These different types of persons often marry each other. What conflicts might develop? How do they resolve leisure time conflicts? Hint: Remember to "give the gift of your opposition."

It is important for both of you to have fun in your leisure time. And it is important to allocate some of your leisure time for service or church-related projects. More about this later.

Discussion Questions:
1. Discuss your individual leisure time interests. How are they different or alike?

2. What do you like to do together for leisure time activities?

3. How might you resolve differences in the ways you spend your leisure time?

Prayer Point/Take Away for Today:
When I have some leisure time, I will evaluate how I use it.

Notes/Responses/Action:

-39-

SERVICE

Read: Mark 12:30–31; Romans 12:6–8, 11; 2 Timothy 1:7;
1 Peter 4:10–11; Hebrews 6:10; 1 Corinthians 12:4

Focus: Christians are serving people.

From the earliest times of the Church, Jesus' followers have been active in helping others. James instructs us that the two facets of the Christian life involve faith and works. He emphasizes works as proof of faith (James 2:24). The Church has sometimes vacillated between stressing faith or works. The facts of scripture clearly let us know that both are to be developed. Everyone, according to St. Paul, has received gifts to use in helping others.

Too often, we make an excuse by listing what we *can't* do! A solution to this is to ask someone who knows us well to help us identify our gifts.

Everyone has gifts, talents, and abilities. The parable of the Good Samaritan (Luke 10:25–37) provides a picture of why we do what we do. Christians are to be living examples of what Christ would do in our shoes. Humanity needs us to be Jesus for them.

Nothing is more attractive to unbelievers than a Christian serving others. And nothing is a better excuse not to believe than a self-centered Christian who avoids using his/her gifts for God.

Discussion Questions:

1. Describe your God-given gifts of service. Be honest; this is not boasting. Be detailed.

2. What are some ways you have used your gifts in the past? How might you use your gifts now and in the future?

3. What gifts do each of you have that could be used in serving others together?

Prayer Point/Take Away for Today:

I will consider the best ways to use my God-given gifts.

Notes/Responses/Action:

(Continued)

Notes/Responses/Action:

-40-

TIME

Read: Philippians 4:6–7; Ecclesiastes 3:1–8; Proverbs 16:9

Focus: Use time wisely.

Each person has an internal clock that goes off at various times. Some people like to be at events, such as church services, at least 15 minutes early. Others are perpetually late or just squeak in the door on time.

Couples with these differences are often identified as having different organizational skills. Some are very organized and easily meet time obligations. Other individuals may be more spontaneous and act as the spirit moves. Of all the irritating contrasts found in couples, the use of time and possession of organizational skills rank high on a regular basis.

Some families develop helpful methods of dealing with tardy individuals' lack of ability to keep appointments. Other families simply honk the horn to speed up those who move slower.

How a couple deals with their differences in organization and time commitments is a topic for ongoing discussion. You can go online and find a myriad of examples dealing with how to increase your time management skills, but that is only part of the solution. Far better it is to admit to each other that you have different internal clocks and decide to adjust to the other's clock.

Both of you may also need to modify some habits. Change in a couple's relationship usually involves a two-way street of alterations of behavior and attitude. Expect change to be a continuing part of life. Believe it or not, change can energize your relationship.

Don't try to transform the other person. That can be an exercise in futility. Lighten up and enjoy the journey you are on together.

Discussion Questions:
1. Describe your tendencies toward being late or overly punctual. Why do you think you are the way you are?

2. Describe your organizational abilities. What similarities do you have in common? How do you differ from each other?

3. How might you adapt to any of these differences?

Prayer Point/Take Away for Today:
I will evaluate my use of time.

Notes/Responses/Action:

(Continued)

Notes/Responses/Action:

-41-

ROLES

Read: Genesis 2:23–24; Ecclesiastes 4:9–11; Amos 3:3; Matthew 18:19

Focus: Be a dynamic duo!

In more traditional cultural settings, there are expectations as to who will do what in the home. Today's Western culture offers a wide range of options with gender often playing less of a role in doing tasks than for prior generations.

The same can be said for decision-making. Each of you has likely come from a family setting where certain roles are understood or assigned. You may or may not be interested in following the same roles as set by your family of origin.

There are a host of detailed tasks to be accomplished in a home. There are also assumptions — often unspoken — about who will do what. These should be thoroughly discussed and worked out, preferably before marriage. Who will cook, or is this a shared activity? How about clearing a table and washing dishes? Laundry? Housecleaning? Vehicle maintenance? Lawn care? Shopping? Child care? Finances (discussed in more detail later)? And the many other home responsibilities that exist!

Each person brings skills to the table that can be utilized or developed. No role is unimportant. Many couples are flexible in their roles. They move back and forth, depending on time commitments and other factors. Taking time to discuss these issues and responsibilities now can help get your future home started well.

Discussion Questions:
1. Describe roles in each of your families of origin.

2. How might each of you decide on your roles as a potentially married couple?

3. What roles do you feel very uncomfortable doing?

4. What roles do you feel comfortable doing?

Prayer Point/Take Away for Today:
I will re-evaluate my view of gender and household roles for my future home.

Notes/Responses/Action:

(Continued)

Notes/Responses/Action:

-42-
DECISION-MAKING AND MONEY

Read: Ecclesiastes 5:10; 1 Timothy 6:17–19; James 1:5

Focus: Develop a wise view of money.

Most of the decisions of life involve money, directly or indirectly. Even whether to have children or how many to have is a financial decision, considering the costs of raising a family. How you use your vacations is an expense item. Health and exercise also carry a price tag. Insurance of all types is not cheap. The benefits provided by your employer(s) can have a huge impact on your lives.

The list is endless, and the choices you have to make may seem never-ending. This is why you need to discuss before marriage, and as a couple, the many topics related to decision-making.

The process of deciding how to spend or use your resources can be a daunting task. Each of you comes from a different financial background where decisions were made in different ways. This could make you feel uncomfortable.

Some families spend most of their money as it becomes available. Others are tight-fisted and have serious controls on how money departs from their hands. For some, every want is a need, and for others, needs always precede wants. Some live in homes with strict budgets, and others live hand-to-mouth with all available funds spent early in the income cycle.

Joining your different financial backgrounds may be the toughest part of merging into marriage. There are many ways of making decisions as a couple. It is important to be candid during the premarried stage and openly describe your own approach to spending money. Don't hold back your tendencies. Each must understand what the other thinks about money.

What you decide now may need to be adjusted after marriage. Circumstances may require changes you did not expect. This is an important area which may require modification as time goes on. Honestly evaluate what will work for you as a couple. This may be the first time one or both of you has faced such a major financial hurdle. Solve it together, and don't be afraid to change if it doesn't work well.

Of course, you can give all decision-making power to one or the other. This can cause all sorts of anxiety and suppressed issues.

You might try shared decisions. This can be tricky, resulting in a tie vote! You could flip a coin, but that might yield issues because you both have opinions.

As you trust each other more, you may learn to yield to the decision that seems to further your shared goals best. One approach is to take a sheet of paper and divide it into columns with pro and con lists to address both sides of an issue. Sometimes this clarifies the situation and helps in decision-making. Make sure to seek God's direction in the decision you make — before, during, and after your decision.

Discussion Questions:
1. Describe how your family of origin made financial decisions.

2. Describe your comfort level in terms of making decisions, especially financial ones.

3. What financial role do you feel very uncomfortable doing?

4. What financial role do you feel most comfortable doing?

Prayer Point/Take Away for Today:
I will rethink how I relate to and handle financial decision-making.

Notes/Responses/Action:

(Continued)

Notes/Responses/Action:

-43-

FINANCES

Read: Proverbs 3:9–10, 13:11; Hebrews 13:5; Matthew 6:21; Malachi 3:10; 1 Chronicles 29:14

Focus: Be wise in spending, giving, and investing.

In addition to the roles each of you fulfill as a married couple, there is the important domain of financial decision-making. Again, there are age-old traditions that often slide to the background in the modern world. It is important to recognize the skills that each of you brings to your relationship and possible marriage.

The old adage that money is the number one cause of marriage breakups holds some truth. Financial wisdom probably develops or comes to light early in life. Some people are very organized and detail-oriented, while others are haphazard in tracking spending and keeping records. Some are very skilled at handling money, while others spend freely and without as much concern for the details.

If these two types marry each other, this is a prescription for stress! How money is spent is an issue for many marriages. Debt and different views of borrowing can be a big problem. Discuss this thoroughly before marriage. Every set of premarital counseling sessions involves finances. This is a big reason to seek a trained premarital counselor.

There are many approaches to handling financial responsibilities. Here are a few examples.

1. Yield money-handling to the person with the best organizational skills. This way, one person is in charge of paying bills, saving for the future, allocating funds for various purposes, and keeping an eye on expenditures. This way, there is no uncertainty about how resources are used. The other person must give way to the organizer in terms of recordkeeping. For this to work, however, there must be a clear understanding about what is purchased and when. The less organized person may feel stressed because of the lack of spontaneity in the system. To alleviate this problem, couples often allocate some monthly "mad money" for spending without worrying about how it is used.

2. Divide the financial responsibilities. Many options exist. One spouse might be involved with routine bill paying (such as electronic autopayment,) and the other with discretionary spending. This requires very close connections so neither party overspends without the other's being aware and agreeing to changes. Sometimes a couple may keep separate accounts (his money and her money). This divided approach should involve continuous cross-checking to be certain that no area is out of place. Communication is vitally essential.

3. Regardless of the approach, both parties must be aware of the expected responsibilities of each. Periodic sharing of details and expectations is key to a low stress situation.

Today's financial world is a complicated place, and each couple should learn as much as possible so they are working toward common goals and planning effectively for the future: careers, children, retirement, etc. Learn together about how to manage money. There are many useful websites and books on how to deal with finances. Money may not seem to be a romantic subject, but romance can evaporate quickly when financial pressures threaten the relationship.

There are a host of models* to use in deciding how money is spent, but one priority should be common throughout the marital relationship of Christians. All resources are ultimately gifts from God. Appropriate allocation of funds for His purposes (the tithe) is a consistent priority throughout the history of Judaism and Christianity. Those who practice faithful giving testify to the blessing of God on their lives and resources.

Resources (Note: They do not agree on some points!):
*https://www.forbes.com/sites/jenniferwoods/2015/07/06/10-ways-to-prevent-money-from-ruining-your-marriage/#1d208e9e44c9
*https://www.daveramsey.com/blog/the-truth-about-money-and-relationships
*https://www.usatoday.com/story/money/personalfinance/2017/07/05/pros-and-cons-sharing-your-finances-married-couple/438157001/

Discussion Questions:
1. Describe your background in terms of your philosophy of money and how you view money.

2. If you decide to marry, how do you think you might want to handle your resources?

3. Describe your comfort level and priorities concerning giving back to God.

Prayer Point/Take Away for Today:
I will rethink my philosophy of money.

Notes/Responses/Action:

-44-

CONTROLLING MONEY

Read: Deuteronomy 8:18a; Proverbs 11:24; Matthew 7:12

Focus: God gives us the ability to have wealth. Be generous.

Say the word *budget,* and everyone cringes. The mind tends to conjure up a restrictive picture of spending that takes all the fun out of living.

Although all premarital counseling discusses finances and budgeting, there does not have to be agony associated with controlled spending. Why do we have to talk about budgets? The reason is simple. After the wedding, money arguments can quickly set in, especially if the couple has given no prior thought to how money will be spent on a daily basis.

Chaos reigns if income is less than expenditures. The only way to avoid this is to sit down and discuss post-wedding incomes and likely expenses. This requires adding up the fixed expenses you know of and subtracting these from your take-home cash.

Estimate your flexible expenses (variables such as food, clothing, entertainment, etc.) and subtract them from the remaining income.

If the residue is positive, pat yourself on the back. If negative, then flexible expenses need your attention.

This requires serious work by both of you. Always include a line item that has no purpose other than however you each want to spend it (mad money). Whatever method you decide to use to keep track of your income/expenses, both of you must agree and take part. Each must know what is going on and have a significant say in the decisions.

Resources: See the resources in the previous devotional.

Discussion Questions:
1. Describe your personal experiences with controlling finances.

2. What sort of financial benefits would you anticipate your employer providing? How might this impact your approach to financial decisions?

3. Describe your thoughts about using a budget as a method of financial control.

Prayer Point/Take Away for Today:
I will evaluate the value of a budget.

Notes/Responses/Action:

(Continued)

Notes/Responses/Action:

-45-

STAYING IN LOVE

Read: Ephesians 4:2–3; Galatians 6:10

Focus: Be consistently in love.

Relationships do not run on air. You must continually nourish each other and thrive on love vitamins. You have probably seen your fair share of TV/movie/theater examples of how a marriage can grind to a halt. The reasons are many: poor money management, lack of attention to each other, a boring lifestyle, unsatisfied sexual needs, outside distractions, family issues, health concerns, and a host of other problems.

The attention of a man pursuing a woman as a marriage partner is sometimes described in this way. He is running after a moving bus, exerting a lot of effort. Once he jumps on the bus, he sits down in a seat, breathes a sigh of relief, and relaxes. The rest of marriage is a dull ride on the bus! He has caught his ride, so what else is there to do?

On the other side, a woman may do quite a bit to be alluring until she lands her man. Then she may relax and go about life in a routine manner, letting her appearance deteriorate. Too often, these two models illustrate many marriages. Each spouse has nothing more to do because the match is done.

Studies of successful marriages that do not follow this dreary tedium find quite the opposite approach. Men and women who are continually attentive to each other and their needs almost

147

universally maintain love at a level that keeps the love vitamins flowing!

A huge diversity exists within successful marriages in terms of details, but many features show up again and again. Successful couples almost never take each other for granted. They generally maintain a sense of attraction for each other by ways that their spouse understands using his/her love language. Refer to the five love languages on Day 28 for keeping the spark going.

Domination by one or the other spouse rarely shows up in happy marriages; equality is the priority. They tend to share responsibilities and decision-making.

Age seems to have little impact on happy marriages. After interviewing happy couples married for 60, 70, or more years, I have observed a growth of mature love that kept them attuned to each other.

The statistics of divorce can be discouraging, but they are often misquoted.* Divorce rates have been falling for many years. The often misquoted 40–50 percent rate is questionable. The actual number is apparently lower than this range. Second and third marriages often fare worse than first marriages, but the often quoted statistics also appear to be significantly inflated. If statistics tend to frighten you away from a marital commitment, here is a truth. *Statistics work only for groups, not on an individual basis.* You can decide (remember the gift of free choice God gives you) to avoid becoming a divorce statistic!

Happiness is essentially a decision you make. Agree together to be successful. Individuals who focus on making their spouses happy and fulfilled are almost never part of the dismal stats!

Resource:
The Good News About Marriage, Shaunti Feldhahn,
WaterBrook Multnomah books.

Discussion Questions:
1. What drew you together in the first place?

2. What can you do to maintain your love relationship?

3. What is your biggest concern in growing your relationship?

Prayer Point/Take Away for Today:
I will do something to grow our relationship.

Notes/Responses/Action:

(Continued)

Notes/Responses/Action:

-46-

TOGETHERNESS

Read: Ecclesiastes 4:9–10; Romans 12:3–5

Focus: Christian married couples are to be one "body."

Happy marriages involve enjoying time together. This is not the hip-joined problem some couples may display.

If you marry, you will need to have connections with friends and organizations outside the home; but these must not distract you from your primary connectivity with your significant other. Plan times to be together, without distractions.

If money is tight and children are involved, this may require careful planning and creativity. Couples sometimes share child care while they have special times by themselves. Married couples sometimes find that they must arrange togetherness without leaving home. This requires saving enough energy and time to withdraw to a spot where they can focus on each other.

Spending money is not a necessity to grow a strong relationship. The decision to be together is the key component.

As premarrieds, you need to find places to simply stare into each other's eyes and talk. Your friends are important for your social lives, but some discussions require your undivided attention. Togetherness is a necessity through all of life.

After marriage, couples sometimes decide to set aside money for a shared vacation as a source of rejuvenation in their relationship. The busyness of life can sap energy and leave little time to share, dream, and let each other know how much they care.

Time is the most important commodity that everyone has. The wise use of this resource together is fundamental to a strong relationship.

Discussion Questions:
1. How do you spend time together? Are you spending enough time in meaningful talk?

2. How do you think you might spend time together if you marry?

3. You are busy people. How do you find time for each other now?

4. How do you think you would deal with health issues?

Prayer Point/Take Away for Today:
I will find time to talk with her/him.

Notes/Responses/Action:

(Continued)

Notes/Responses/Action:

-47-

SEX AND ALL THAT STUFF!

Read: Hebrews 13:4; Proverbs 5:18–20; 1 Corinthians 7:3–5

Focus: Wait for marital sex!

Our Western society is, to say the least, sex-saturated. Check the list of current movies for their ratings: R often dominates with explicit sex between unmarried couples frequently portrayed. The message is that a normal couple will have sex after a first or certainly after the second date.

This sad state portrays sex as something that men and women do just for fun with no strings attached. God never intended this distortion of His wonderful creation.

St. Paul lived in a sex-dominated society as well. Prostitution occurred in pagan temple worship. Sex was literally part of some groups' religion! Paul sounded a clear alarm and referred back to the original plan of God that sex be limited to committed marriage because of the intimate nature of the relationship.

The oneness that is biologically and psychologically built into sexual love is unique among humans, compared to simple copulation in the rest of the organic world. The media portrays sex as just a casual thing that is no more than personal physical satisfaction and adventure. The hedonistic idea is that sex comes first, before marriage. This is the antithesis of Christian marriage.

Arranged marriages have been around far longer than today's self-centered approach to marriage. In those marriages, commitment preceded sex, and love developed later. Modern Western society tends to deify love as an all-consuming purpose. In this setting, sex is the trial ground before making a commitment. How many build relationships on this flimsy foundation — and then watch them crumble?

The stability of civilizations has been tied to families. Sexually transmitted diseases would be almost non-existent if there was no promiscuity.

The church has a huge responsibility to call everyone to a life free of premarital sex. This is not popular, but Christianity was never intended to be popular. The benefits of sexual restraints until marriage far outweigh the issues that arise when living with a boyfriend/girlfriend. Live-in couples experience problems akin to marriage issues but without the commitment to resolve those issues through prior preparation. Jumping to the next bedroom solves nothing. Trial sex runs do not deal with the issues that premarital counseling can help resolve.

Make a commitment to refrain from sexual intimacy until the "I do" is complete. This helps you avoid regret.

Before marriage, each of you needs to have a physical exam, for your own knowledge and safety. Learn about family planning and begin to think about what you are comfortable with. Discussions with a premarital counselor can be very helpful.

Once inside the marital relationship, the restraints are gone. Refer to some excellent Christian books on sexual techniques.* In marriage, you can fully enjoy each other.

Resource:
The Gift of Sex, Clifford and Joyce Penner, Word Publishing.

Discussion Questions:
1. Describe your understanding of sexual intimacy. Where did you learn this?

2. What are the benefits of postponing sexual intimacy until marriage?

3. How will you postpone sexual intimacy until marriage?

Prayer Point/Take Away for Today:
I will postpone sexual intimacy until marriage.

Notes/Responses/Action:

(Continued)

Notes/Responses/Action:

-48-

ROMANTIC MYTH

Read: Proverbs 4:23–27

Focus: Stay focused on what is important.

Lurking below the surface, and fed by the media, is a common and dangerous myth about couple relationships: "There is someone out there who can make me happy all my life, without much effort on my part." To those sucked into this whirlpool of mythology, marriage can come as a jarring reality. Still believing this charade, marriage partners have many reactions:

"I am not happy."

"It must be that I didn't find the 'right' person. Just didn't go to enough singles bars or use enough dating apps."

"My spouse must not be trying hard enough."

This dissatisfaction can lead to emotional adultery where she/he finds someone else (at work, etc.) to meet those emotional needs. The next step can be a physical affair, followed by a nasty divorce which leaves scars that may never quite heal. Remarriage too soon due to inadequate grieving may lead to another divorce. And the cycle repeats!

To break the myth of perfection apart may require the aid of a mentor or counselor or pastor. Wise counsel often recommends that couples return to patterns and behaviors that used to work; in other words, learn to love each other again.*

Amazing stories come from those who give up the myth and do the hard work of developing a relationship built not on sex alone or on easy solutions, but on the desire and commitment to love a person for who they are.

The idea of marrying for romantic reasons dates only from the 18th century in Western society. Today's media often portray romance as a necessity for a meaningful relationship. Since romance is an emotional thing, depending on emotions as the sole basis to maintain a wonderful marriage is faulty.

As a premarried couple, you can benefit by focusing on the total person you might marry, not on some limited view of who she/he is. Instead, take a holistic view of each other and pay attention to the idea of love language discussed earlier. Romance can be related to love language. In other words, if you focus on the love needs of each other, romance may tag along as an added benefit!

Resource:
Divorce Busting, Michele Weiner-Davis, Fireside, Simon and Schuster.

Discussion Questions:
1. Describe your concept of romance.

2. Describe relational myths you have seen in the media or heard from friends or which you have had, as appropriate.

3. How can you, as a couple, work toward a realistic romantic view of each other and the relationship you hope to develop?

Prayer Point/Take Away for Today:
This week, I will surprise him/her with something he/she recognizes as romantic.

Notes/Responses/Action:

-49-
WHAT IS LOVE?

Read: Ephesians 5:21–33; 1 Corinthians 13

Focus: Love covers a lot of territory.

You know the soppy, dewy-eyed view of love portrayed on TV, in movies, and in romance novels: you will automatically know that this is the one. This idea pervades much of American society.

But what happens when the rose-colored glasses break or dissolve, and your stomach doesn't have the quivers anymore? Do you fall out of love just as quickly as you fell in love? Or how about the all too common excuse: "I don't love you anymore"? These all reflect a view that love is a feeling, that you will know and recognize love automatically.

So, what about the couple who has all the right feelings while dating and, after marriage, their feelings go down the tubes? They find themselves living in a wretched existence without those wonderful sensations they knew before. Is there more to love than having the right vibrations?

Let's look at the kinds of love defined by the Greeks and found in the New Testament:*

1. *Eros*: Erotic love is the love associated with male-female attraction and is related to sex.

2. *Philia*: Friendship love refers to those with whom we have close communication and share our inner thoughts.

3. *Storge*: Family love is not used in the New Testament but refers to the bonds that hold families together.

4. *Agape*: Divine love or Christian love, as described in 1 Corinthians 13, is selfless love that looks out for the best in someone else.

In Ephesians 5:25, St. Paul says that husbands are to show this sacrificial Christian love (*agape*) to their wives. In the culture of Paul's day, wives were already expected to do this. So Paul brings wives and husbands to the same level by requiring husbands to be *agape* lovers.

In Ephesians 5:21, Paul casts an umbrella over the succeeding verses, which is often misunderstood in our culture, misused to suggest dominance, and has led to abuse.**

Agape love is the goal for Christian couples. How different is 1 Corinthians 13 from the strictly erotic love foisted onto Americans by the media. Certainly there is erotic love in a male-female relationship, but *agape* love depends on care and commitment instead of feelings! Erotic love may draw you together, but *agape* love transforms your relationship into a beautiful bond that the pagan world knows nothing about. Go for the *agape*!

Resources:
**Easy to Live With*, Leslie Parrott, Beacon Hill Press of Kansas City.
**https://www.focusonthefamily.com/family-q-and-a/relationships-and-marriage/submission-of-wives-to-husbands

Discussion Questions:
1. Read 1 Corinthians 13 aloud together and discuss how this transforms our American view of marriage.

2. What can you do to begin to have *agape* love in your relationship?

3. How important might *philia* love be in your relationship?

Prayer Point/Take Away for Today:
I will think of some ways to show *agape* love to him/her.

Notes/Responses/Action:

(Continued)

Notes/Responses/Action:

-50-

CRITICISM

Read: Proverbs 14:29; Romans 12:19

Focus: Keep a lid on critical talk.

TV family humor often centers on criticism of various members of the family. This may be funny, but where does criticism fit into a love relationship? Criticism is focused on someone's weaknesses, which we all have. Nobody is without flaws, and some are quite glaring.

Do we know that we have flaws? Most of us are quite aware of our own weaknesses and failures. We don't really have to be told about them to make us aware of their existence. Criticism is essentially a negative experience.

Negative experiences dominate our lives in the real world. We really do not need to have our significant others pour more negativity on us. What do we need? All the research tells us that positives are what we need to counter the negative influences.* This is not the same as the "everybody wins" stuff that affects some areas of sports. We need to tell the truth; but the *emphasis* is on what we do right, not on our known-to-us weaknesses. A couple who communicates effectively has learned that the best way to approach a problem is to help lift the burden, rather than to increase the weight.

When approaching a sensitive issue, use the magic "I" word to remove the antagonistic "you" word from your talks.

When describing how a behavior makes one feel, the onus shifts to a discussion of what will help, instead of raising resentment with an attack to a sore spot. "I feel ill-at-ease when I sense that you are angry with me for ___," is far better than "You always get angry when ___."

The object is not to ignore a problem but to approach it in a non-threatening way, if possible. When tempted to be critical, pause and think about the anticipated reaction of your significant other upon hearing your snide comment. Easy does it. Leave criticism to the sit-coms!

Resource:
Why Marriages Succeed or Fail, John Gottman, Fireside, Simon and Schuster.

Discussion Questions:
1. Practice using "I" statements to express issues you have with each other.

2. How can you go out of your way to be non-critical with each other?

Prayer Point/Take Away for Today:
I will use "I" statements instead of "you" statements when things get tense between us.

Notes/Responses/Action:

(Continued)

Notes/Responses/Action:

-51-

SAY WHAT'S IMPORTANT

Read: Galatians 6:2; 1 Peter 1:22

Focus: Carry the other person's burdens.

How do you say what is important in your relationship? First of all, be clear. Each of us sees things differently, so share your vision and lift your discussion to a new level. Say what is important to you. Build on your strengths.*

For example, a wonderful conversation might begin with: "I want you to know how important our relationship is to me." Then go on to describe what this means to you. You might increase your connection with her/him by sharing your vision of what your relationship might grow into. This can keep your conversation from becoming boring or repetitious.

Philip Yancey makes this cogent statement: "... the very differences ... personality, outlook, and daily routine — actually represent a great strength. Janet provides me with a new set of eyes into a world I barely know about ... I marvel at the differences in temperament and spiritual gifts that allow her to spend her day dealing with situations that would probably drive me crazy."**

Resources:
Empowering Couples, 2nd edition, David H. Olson and Amy K. Olson, Life Innovations, Inc.
**Grace Notes*, Philip Yancey, Zondervan.

Discussion Questions:

1. What topics can you discuss that you haven't dealt with before?

2. How can you increase the level of your conversations?

Prayer Point/Take Away for Today:

I will do my best to say some things that are important to me about our relationship, but I will say them gently and with grace.

Notes/Responses/Action:

(Continued)

Notes/Responses/Action:

-52-
THE "MAGIC QUESTION"

Read: Proverbs 31:10–11; Ephesians 5:25

Focus: Be respectful and sacrificial toward each other.

Let's say that you sense something is bothering your significant other. How do you approach her/him to help? There are many things you could say to assist the discussion. Here is one that is almost universally applicable: **"What do you need from me right now?"** This can often loosen the logjam of feelings that are bottled up within her/him. Perhaps she/he can then open up and reveal what is bothering her/him.

Be prepared to empathize as best you can. In some circumstances, silence may be more important than what you say. Listen carefully. Don't try to heal or repair. She/he may tell you what is going on. If not, don't despair. Quietness may be what is most essential at this specific time. Be ready to give the gift of silent presence.

Discussion Questions:
1. How might the "magic question" help her/him?

2. When might you have used this in your relationship?

3. Why would the "magic question" be important to us?

Prayer Point/Take Away for Today:
I will be sensitive to her/his feelings.

Notes/Responses/Action:

-53-

FAMILY ISSUES

Read: Psalm 68:6a; 1 Timothy 5:8

Focus: Family traditions are important.

Those who work with couples generally agree that when you marry, you do indeed marry a family. As a couple, you cannot escape your backgrounds. You can choose which parts of your background that you wish to keep or reject in your new relationship, but the past colors your life, one way or another.

Don't despair over this. Learn to use past family backgrounds as a backdrop for making decisions in the new family you are thinking about forming. Deal with the bad. Keep the good.

Differences between families are numerous. A host of unique differences include: how and when food is prepared versus eating out, entertainment permissions or requirements, discipline of children, sleep habits, chores, work patterns, spiritual training, hygiene, and lots of different expectations and assumed responsibilities. A discussion of the expectations and responsibilities you see in your future home is important, since this is the stuff of everyday life.

Newly married couples have many family issues to face. One source of stress is the issue of which family traditions to follow. For example, where will you spend holidays? Will you alternate between families for Thanksgiving and Christmas celebrations? Families have many common expectations of you as a couple: "Of course you will be here on Christmas Eve, since we always open presents then, right?"

Be aware that working out two or more family patterns can make you feel pulled in many directions. Finding your own way in your new family will be critical to resolving these issues. Even before marriage, let your families enjoy you as a couple while you develop your own traditions as you work things out together. You are forming a new family culture. Build on the strengths each of you brings to the relationship.*

Resource:
Empowering Couples, 2nd edition, David H. Olson and Amy K. Olson, Life Innovations, Inc.

Discussion Questions:
1. Talk about your family expectations at holiday times.

2. How might you work out conflicts between holiday schedules of your families?

3. What will you say to parents, grandparents, or whomever when you have to make a decision that seems to cut across their expectations?

Prayer Point/Take Away for Today:
I will ask about any holiday traditions that we should discuss and be sensitive to her/his family traditions.

Notes/Responses/Action:

(Continued)

Notes/Responses/Action:

-54-

FRIENDS

Read: Proverbs 27:9, 13:20

Focus: Choose friends wisely.

As a single person, you no doubt have special friends, people you may have known for long or short periods of time. They are individuals you enjoy being around and sharing time with. Perhaps they feel free to pop in on you at random times. After marriage, one of the surprises which many couples face is the sudden shift of friendships. For example, popping in randomly may not be appropriate and could be quite embarrassing!

An unofficial survey of newly married couples will probably include a shock like this: "I haven't seen my best man since the wedding! What's with that?" Or "She and I used to hang out all the time, but now we seem to have drifted away. What happened?" The singles world of the past tends to fade into the background as you establish your marital relationship. Time that you previously spent with friends is now devoted to your spouse.

Also, as a dating or married person, you may feel more comfortable in a group of couples. New couple friendships develop. This is perfectly normal, but there can be hurt feelings on the part of your good single friends. Do your best to make the shift as easy as possible for them, but they need to understand that things are different now. You have a new priority structure. Your significant other is number one on your list of humans.

Discussion Questions:
1. Describe any changes that might occur between you and your friends if marriage approaches.

2. What changes do you anticipate happening with friends, if you marry?

Prayer Point/Take Away for Today:
I will think about how my friends interact with us and consider how this might change if we marry.

Notes/Responses/Action:

(Continued)

Notes/Responses/Action:

-55-

EXPECTATIONS

Read: Joshua 1:9; Romans 5:3–5; 1 Peter 5:7

Focus: Let God guide your future.

Everyone entering marriage has expectations. No one anticipates an unhappy marriage. No one thinks there will a disastrous divorce. Most are wearing glasses that are at least slightly rose- tinted. And that is how it should be. But if a married couple is harmed by divorce, then something happened between "I do" and "I'm out of here!"

Plenty of studies try to tease out what slams the door on *happy* and admits *sadness* into the relationship. Probably most important is to look first at what makes happy marriages work. One of the top items is how a couple communicates with each other.* This involves being open and honest, while maintaining full respect, and includes looking level-eyed at each other (seeing each other as equals and affirming that nobody in this relationship is below the other). Happy couples tend to express an abundance of positive feelings, along with a willingness to apologize for mistakes. We could stop there because such an approach leaves petty differences and selfishness in the dust.

Learning to communicate with the opposite gender in an atmosphere of love and acceptance will trump almost everything else in a couple relationship. Getting to this level of communication is not easy, since we all have baggage that can shortcut our higher goals.

The main point: Other issues can usually be resolved if we strive for a deep level of communication saturated with respect, positive feelings, and apologies.

Resource:
The Relationship Cure, John M. Gottman and Joan DeClaire, Crown Publishers.

Discussion Questions:
1. What is your greatest skill in communicating with each other?

2. How can you improve your communication skills?

Prayer Point/Take Away for Today:
I will do my best to upgrade my communication level with her/him.

Notes/Responses/Action:

(Continued)

Notes/Responses/Action:

-56-

GOALS

Read: Romans 8:28; Philippians 3:12–14

Focus: Never stop moving forward.

Everyone has goals or directions he/she wants his/her life to take. So, a couple planning to enter life together will discover that each has an individual set of goals. These goals may not be a perfect match, and that is fully normal.

A couple thinking about marriage needs to list their personal goals and what each hopes to see their future look like together. Melding these various sets of personal goals and couple or family goals is not a trivial task.

As your relationship develops toward marriage, discussions about goals should remain high on your agenda. This should be the beginning of a process of evaluation and setting of priorities that will continue throughout your life together.

There needs to be lots of give and take. Nobody's goal is above another's. All goals may not carry equal weight, but all must be heard and discussed. Take your time. This is not a quick process. It certainly is not an easy process, either. Cover your discussions with prayer. Allow God's Spirit to guide you.

Enjoy the excitement of mutual goal setting! And revisit your goals often. They will likely change as time progresses.

Discussion Questions:
1. List your personal goals. Then compare your lists. How alike or unlike are your personal goals?

2. Depending on how far along you are in your relationship, discuss goals you might anticipate together.

Prayer Point/Take Away for Today:
I will re-evaluate my personal goals in light of our relationship.

Notes/Responses/Action:

(Continued)

Notes/Responses/Action:

-57-

PREMARITAL COUNSELING

Read: Proverbs 8:14; Proverbs 15:22

Focus: Seek help when needed.

The data are clear: the more thorough the premarital counseling experience, the greater a couple's marital happiness. This should be no surprise. A well-trained premarital counselor who uses a professionally developed premarital assessment tool is a valuable asset in helping you to explore the full range of factors that are part of the marriage relationship. This person might be a pastor or counselor or lay counselor at a church.

Prior to the beginning of premarital counseling, most counselors will administer a set of assessment questions that have been developed to cover the topics found in premarital counseling. There are various instruments which the counselor might use. There may be a small fee for the assessment.

Professional counselors will typically charge a fee per session. Pastors may or may not charge. This might depend if the couple is part of her/his congregation. Most sessions typically last from a half-hour to an hour. There is no given number of sessions that you can expect, although between four to six meetings might be common.

Premarital counseling should not be scary. The purpose is to help you explore the great variety of concerns that couples may deal with in a secure, confidential, and comfortable setting.

When to begin premarital counseling can vary. Running in just two weeks before the wedding is not at all desirable! The pressure of wedding preparations is often a huge distraction and may blunt the value of the experience. An ideal time might be as soon as you decide to become serious about the future of your life together.

A thorough premarital counseling series may generate some serious questions that require answering. The willingness of you and your significant other to make appropriate changes is key to making the counseling work. Enjoy the experience! Prepare to grow.

Many churches offer programs which pair a premarried couple with a mentor couple. This provides support and a safe environment to discuss issues and concerns.

Discussion Questions:
1. Are you interested in premarital counseling right now? If not, when might you be interested?

2. Who might be an appropriate premarital counselor? How about a mentor couple?

Prayer Point/Take Away for Today:
When we get serious about exploring a marriage relationship, we will seek premarital counseling.

Notes/Responses/Action:

(Continued)

Notes/Responses/Action:

-58-

WRAPPING IT UP

Read: Ecclesiastes 7:8–9

Focus: Go on from here.

"It is easier to start than to finish" (a quote from Carol Reams, my wife). Preparing for marriage is not for wimps. Happy relationships do not just happen; they are the result of a couple's attentiveness to each other and seeking the best for each other. God wants the best for you. That means deciding to stick with the process to become the best soulmates you can be.

As you have worked through the discussion questions in this series of devotionals, hopefully you have discovered more about each other and more about your God who made you. To continue to grow, share devotions and prayer together by using one of the many helpful books and guides available.

If you continue in your relationship and eventually marry, I wish you God's best in the process.

Consider the relationship ladder. Imagine a ladder from the side. You are at one leg, and your significant other is at the other leg. At the top of the ladder is God. Imagine steps on both legs of the ladder. As each of you climbs the ladder, two things happen. You individually become closer to God, and you become closer to each other.

Before Your Journey

Strive to be all that God has in store for you, and move toward a beautiful unity with each other. God wants the best for you. Communicating with Him and with each other is an unbeatable combination!

Discussion Questions:

1. Review what stands out to each of you about what you have learned through these devotionals.

2. Talk about how you want to proceed from here.

Prayer Point/Take Away for Today: I will consider our relationship in the light of God's leading.

Notes/Responses/Action:

(Continued)

Notes/Responses/Action:

-59-
CHILDREN

Read: Psalm 127:3; Proverbs 22:6; Matthew 19:13–15;
Ephesians 6:1–2; Colossians 3:21; Leviticus 19:32;
Deuteronomy 4:9

Focus: Parenting is an important responsibility. Disciplining
children requires care. Bring your children to Jesus.

Deciding to have children is a big decision and not to be
treated casually. If you decide to marry and have children
together, be ready to give them abundant time at all stages of their
lives.

Here is the key: **You never outgrow being a parent!**
From infant to adult, your children are always your children. That
doesn't mean that you treat them as small children all their lives!
There are many phases as you nurse, train, discipline, guide,
release, and encourage independence. There is no magic formula
to follow. Provide a life model that your children can observe and
find attractive.

Each child has her/his own personality, which you should
honor and respect. Discipline should depend on the child's
personality and how a child responds to your approach. There is
no universal solution to a child's resistance! Treat each child
according to what works best for him/her. No two children are
alike; relate to them in ways that honor their uniquenesses.*

Abuse has no place in parenting. Neither does permissive, total freedom, especially in the early years.

Introducing each child to Jesus is critical for their spiritual development. Financial wisdom also begins early in a child's life.

Don't let any of the maturing phases develop randomly. Parenting is not for wimps!

Resource:
Different Children, Different Needs, The Art of Adjustable Parenting, Charles F. Boyd, Multnomah Books.

Comment: If either of you have children, it might be wise to discuss styles of parenting, blending familes, and other concerns with your premarital counselor.

Discussion Questions:
1. Describe your relationship with your parents.

2. What would you like to keep/not keep from your own family background and how your parents raised you?

3. What is your attitude toward raising a child?

Prayer Point/Take Away for Today:
I will re-evaluate my ideas about children and parenting, and then discuss these with her/him.

Notes/Responses/Action:

(Continued)

Notes/Responses/Action:

-60-

Taking the Leap

Read: John 2:1–2

Focus: Jesus was invited to a wedding. Invite Him to your wedding, and He will come.

If you decide to marry, be careful about getting caught up in the rush and preparation for the wedding and forgetting why you are doing all this. Do your best to enjoy the journey! And remember to invite Jesus to your wedding!

Weddings can be extremely expensive: The cost of a wedding in the United States in 2018 depends on the source cited. Average quoted costs range from 25,000 to 45,000. Location is important with huge price differences between major cities and smaller towns. Decisions about rings, number of guests, flowers, etc. can greatly increase or decrease the cost. One source suggests that half of the weddings cost less than $15,000. The resource below can provide a rough estimate.*

Wedding costs do not include any honeymoon expenses. Ask various sources how to keep wedding expenses from getting out of control.

Plan your wedding in terms of the *meaning* behind your marriage, as opposed to how much money you can spend. Many couples write their own wedding vows, reflecting their beliefs and purposes for life and relationship.

Many churches have individuals skilled in helping you through the details of the ceremony and are happy to incorporate your unique ideas and philosophy.

I pray for you a wonderful life with the guidance of God. Live for Him. If you marry, serve Jesus Christ as a unified couple.

Resource:
*https://www.costofwedding.com

Discussion Questions:
1. Describe your thoughts about a wedding.

2. How can you invite Jesus to your wedding?

Prayer Point/Take Away for Today:
Pray together for guidance in our future decisions.

Notes/Responses/Action:

(Continued)

Notes/Responses/Action:

(Continued)

Notes/Responses/Action:

MY PRAYER FOR YOU

Jesus, please give this couple a sense of your presence in their daily lives. May they reflect on your will and depend on your grace to guide them in the decisions they make about their relationship. Help them to see the great potential they have to help bring about your Kingdom on Earth. May love be their underlying principle as they relate to each other. Give your guiding Spirit in such a way that they trust your wisdom throughout their lives. If they marry, may a common faith bind them in love. Help them to be wonderful examples of people who serve you.

In your great Name, Amen

ABOUT THE AUTHOR

Max W. Reams, B.A., B.S., M.S., M.P.C. (Master of Pastoral Counseling), Ph.D., LL.D. (honorary) is married to Carol A. (Cushard) Reams, A.A., B.S., M.P.C. They have three children, five grandchildren, and great-grandchildren, too. He taught 50 years at Olivet Nazarene University. He is a Trainer for Life Innovation, Inc. (Prepare-Enrich premarital/marital assessment). He is a Certified Life Coach. He and Carol are Volunteer Chaplains. They have led numerous retreats for married couples and worked with many premarital and married couples.

Made in the
USA
Lexington, KY